Anatomy of the Crash

Anatomy of the Crash

The Financial Crisis of 2020

EDITED BY
THO BISHOP

INTRODUCTION BY
JEFF DEIST

MISESINSTITUTE
AUBURN, ALABAMA

Mises Institute
518 West Magnolia Ave.
Auburn, Ala. 36832
mises.org
contact@mises.org

ISBN: 978-1-61016-722-2

Contents

Preface

by Tho Bishop

"End the Fed!" Three small words became one of the most improbable and powerful political chants in modern politics thanks to the presidential campaigns of Dr. Ron Paul. With the backdrop of a global financial crisis, the congressman from Texas was able to use the microphone of modern politics, forever changed by the internet and social media, to wake up a generation of Americans to the threat posed by central banks and fiat money. Ideological gatekeepers in Washington and the corporate press found themselves forced to recognize and attack a previously obscure school of economic thought that was now being talked about by college students, activists, and even the odd politician.

Of course, no such movements ever truly happen overnight. The seeds of the international Austrian revival were planted when Ludwig von Mises escaped World War II Europe and made a home for himself in America. With positions at New York University and the Foundation for Economic Education, Mises was able to develop a legion of followers in both academia and the public at large. Several students of his NYU seminar, such as Israel Kirzner, Hans Sennholz, and Ralph Raico, became important Austrian scholars in their own right. It was, however, Murray Rothbard who was perhaps Mises's most significant mentee, with not only significant contributions to economics, history, and political philosophy, but popular writings aimed at energizing a grassroots Austro-libertarian movement far outside the restraints of the ivory tower.

Rothbard's potent blend of serious scholarship and dynamic popularism became a model for the Mises Institute, which he helped found with Lew Rockwell in 1982. Since the beginning, the Institute has been both an incubator for new generations of Austrian scholars and a fount of education for the public at large.

Anyone who is familiar with the works of Mises, Rothbard, and the Austrian school understands how far removed they are from the progressive-dominated *zeitgeist* that has long controlled the most powerful microphones of the West. Although this carries with it the curse of limiting the influence that it could have with policymakers in government, it also means that it benefits from times when the public questions the very foundations of the institutions that it was indoctrinated to believe in.

Two thousand eight was such a time. Unfortunately, 2020 appears to be one as well.

The purpose of this collection is to highlight the important work of contemporary Austrian economists on the modern financial system. Although the mainstream financial press has been crediting American, European, and Chinese policymakers with upholding the global economy in the aftermath of 2008, Austrians have long been warning that these very same actions have only set the world up for a larger disaster. Promises in 2008 of the ease of normalizing monetary policy—such as by reducing balance sheets and phasing out market intervention—have been proven to be lies, just as Austrians warned.

While the government response to the coronavirus may serve as a catalyst for the next crisis, it is the irresponsible actions of central bankers, governments, and globalist institutions that will make the pain so much more intense. Worse still, the response will be led by individuals who are only versed in the same failed ideologies that brought us to where we are now.

The first section is a look back at major policy decisions that brought us to where we are now. One of the important aims of this collection is to highlight the truly global nature of these failings, not simply critiquing the actions of the Federal Reserve, but their colleagues at the European Central Bank, the Bank of Japan, and elsewhere. It is the coordinated attempt by central bankers around the world to try to bolster markets by hiding and mispricing underlying financial risk that has only served to escalate the fragility of the global economy.

This is followed by a look forward to what we might expect from policymakers as they are forced to respond. The combined fiscal and monetary response to the coronavirus and the government-imposed lockdown has highlighted the degree to which central bankers and modern governments feel completely unhampered by concerns about inflation or government debt. Every attempt will be made to prop up the financial bubbles they have created, and these actions will only compound the fundamental issues we face. Of course, as economic decision-makers become ever more drastic in their thought, we can expect them to resort more to using the full authoritarian powers of the modern state.

Lastly, the book looks at placing the ideas of the Austrian school within the context of the modern world. Although questions of underlying ideology may be dismissed by "practical" individuals who pride themselves on being "independent thinkers," Mises understood the degree to which our intellectual environment directly guides policy and institutional frameworks. In the aftermath of the challenging times that may be ahead, the only way to build a stronger, more prosperous, and more stable future will be with an ideological revolution.

I hope that you will find this collection of articles enlightening, even if the ramifications of their content mean difficulty in the short term.

Introduction

by Jeff Deist

The Great Crash of 2020 was not caused by a virus. It was *precipitated* by the virus, and made worse by the crazed decisions of governments around the world to shut down business and travel. But it was *caused* by economic fragility. The supposed greatest economy in US history actually was a walking sick man, made comfortable with painkillers, and looking far better than he felt—yet ultimately fragile and infirm. The coronavirus pandemic simply exposed the underlying sickness of the US economy. If anything, the crash was overdue.

Too much debt, too much malinvestment, and too little honest pricing of assets and interest rates made America uniquely vulnerable to economic contagion. Most of this vulnerability can be laid at the feet of central bankers at the Federal Reserve, and we will pay a terrible price for it in the coming years. This is an uncomfortable truth, one that central bankers desperately hope to obscure while the media and public remain fixated on the virus.

But we should not let them get away with it, because (at least when it comes to legacy media) the Fed's gross malfeasance is perhaps the biggest untold story of our lifetimes.

Symptoms of problems were readily apparent just last September during the commercial bank repo crisis. After more than a decade of quantitative easing, relentless interest rate cutting, and huge growth in "excess" reserves (more than $1.5 trillion) parked at the Fed, banks still did not have enough overnight liquidity? The repo market exposed how banks were capital contstrained, not reserve constrained. So what exactly was the point of taking the Fed's balance sheet from less than $1 trillion to over $4 trillion, anyway? Banks still needed money, after a decade of QE?

As with most crises, the problems took root decades ago. What we might call the era of modern monetary policy took root with the 1971 Nixon Shock, which eliminated any convertibility of dollars for gold. Less than twenty years later, in October 1987, Black Monday wiped out 20 percent of US stock market valuations. Fed chair Alan Greenspan promised Wall Street that such a thing would never happen again on his watch, and he meant it: the "Greenspan Put" was the Maestro's blueprint for providing as much monetary easing as needed to prop up equity markets. The tech stock crash of the NASDAQ in 2000 only solidified the need for "new" monetary policy, and in 2008 that policy took full flight under the obliging hand of Fed chairman Ben Bernanke—a man who not only fundamentally misunderstood the Great Depression in his PhD thesis, but who also had the self-regard to write a book titled *The Courage to Act* about his use of other people's money to reinflate the biggest and baddest stock bubble in US history.

In response to the coronavirus crisis, at least ostensibly, both the Fed and the US Treasury went into hyperdrive during March of 2020. The Fed's response to the crash strains credulity, simply because it has been so brazen. In fact any article about the Fed becomes obsolete in just a few days, as it announces new programs, credit facilities, and purchases at a dizzying pace. In just the past six weeks the Fed announced $700 billion in new rounds of asset purchases from banks, to the point where the financial press has lost count of which "round" of quantitative easing.

But more QE was just the beginning. Fed officials also cut the Federal Funds rate to nearly zero, and announced that bank reserve ratio requirements would be eliminated as of March 2020. This puts a new twist on fractional reserve banking, because it is hard to have a fraction when the numerator is zero...

Apart from this, the Fed also initiated a $1.5 trillion program of short-term lending facilities, with borrowers providing as collateral anything from Treasury debt to commercial paper to securities backed by student loans, auto loans, and credit-card loans. But there is more: for the first time in history, the Fed will spend billions purchasing corporate bonds, perhaps the biggest bubble of all in an economy full of debt-laden companies which took advantage of cheap interest rates to buy back equity and generally substitute financial engineering for real growth. Helpfully, the Fed chose the world's biggest asset management firm to run the corporate debt purchase program through various Exchange Traded Funds. And that firm, BlackRock, happens to be the world's largest provider of said ETFs.

As a result of all this, the Fed's balance sheet already has surged to over $6 trillion in mid-April 2020, and can anyone doubt it will soon be $10 trillion? Meanwhile, Congress managed to get involved with monetary policy through the back-door in its $2 trillion "stimulus" bill called the CARES Act. The Act contains $454 billion to back an entirely separate Fed loan program for banks and corporations, a sum the Fed can leverage up to 10X or $4.5 trillion. This is done using a "special purpose vehicle" under the auspices of the Treasury Department. This represents the melding of fiscal and monetary policy, the unholy blurring of any distinction (much less independence) of the Fed relative to Congress and the executive. It also represents the potential for another huge spike in the Fed's balance sheet.

Of course neither Congress nor the Fed can get the nation's fiscal house in order, no matter how much they print and spend. In fact, the 2020 federal deficit is projected at $4 trillion, which would represent more than 100 percent of likely tax revenue! $1,200 relief checks from the CARES Act will not go far when people are prohibited from working, and very little of the bill's spending will trickle down to individual Americans. The cascading effect across retail business and restaurants, landlords and mortgage companies, the travel industry, and local tax revenue will be overwhelming.

As this economic crisis unfolds, we will know the Fed has lost control if one of two things happen:

First, if the influx of new money and credit so rapidly created by the Fed causes (or at least worsens) rapid price inflation for consumers. Unlike 2008, this new money creation is not going primarily into the monetary base as commercial bank reserves. It is flowing out across the range of Fed purchases, and already in January and February the M2 money stock grew more than 15 percent. In 2008 economists of an Austrian bent warned, correctly, that a vast and sudden expansion of the Fed's balance sheet would have very harmful consequences. They were derided when hyperinflation did not materialize, but in fact there has been significant price inflation across a range of assets. Since the Fed has opened the floodgates far wider than in 2008, and since the residual effects of aggressive monetary easing since 2008 are still felt across markets, significant consumer price inflation is a real concern. If prices begin to rise noticeably, we will know the Fed has lost the ability to push off the day of reckoning.

Second, look for hiccups in the market for US Treasury debt which has implicitly relied on Fed backing since 2008. The Fed's willingness to buy up Treasuries in huge numbers from commercial banks signals to the world it will always act as a backstop and "make the market" as needed. Ultra-low interest rates engineered by the Fed ensure that debt service does not grow too large in the annual federal budget—less than $500 billion annually at present. This keeps Congress happy, knowing they can spend wildly beyond tax revenues without much pain. But this is perverse: if investors know the Fed will buy assets at a certain price no matter what markets do, they are not buying an "investment" but rather a guaranteed upside with socialized losses—every hapless dollar holder becomes a *de facto* surety for US Treasuries.

But what if they held a Treasury auction and no one bid? What if demand weakens, especially as Uncle Sam pays less than 1 percent interest on a ten-year bond? What if foreign buyers, representing almost 40 percent of US debt held by the public, simply lose faith that the profligate US government will ever get its fiscal house in order? If the Fed became the *primary* buyer at auction, that too would send a signal to the world—and a bad one. Rising interest rates for Treasury debt would be a calamity for the federal government budget, as even historically average rates above 5 percent would spike debt service above $1 trillion annually. The entire inflationary program, using monetary stimulus to prop up flagging demand, is utterly dependent on a steady market for US debt paying near zero interest. From Keynes to Krugman, this is the program. But like a game of musical chairs, nobody wants to hold low-yield Treasuries if rates begin to rise no matter what the Fed does.

So what now? What should we make of the Fed today?

James Grant of *Grant's Interest Rate Observer* characterizes the Fed's recent actions as a "leveraged buy-out of the United States of America." The Fed is assumed to have an unlimited balance sheet, able to provide financial markets with "liquidity" as needed, in any amount, for any length of time. Pennsylvania senator Pat Toomey urges the Fed to do more, and Congress to spend more, all in the unholy name of liquidity.

But liquidity is nothing more than ready money for investment and spending. In the current environment it is a euphemism for free manna from heaven. It is "free" money—unearned, representing no increase in output or productivity. It has no backing and no redeemability. And not only are there no new goods and services in the economy, there are far fewer due to the lockdown.

So monetary "policy" as we know it is dead as a doornail. What central banks and Fed officials do no longer falls within the realm of economics or policy; in fact the Fed no longer operates as what we think of as a central bank. It is not a back-stop or "banker's bank," as originally designed (in theory), nor is it a steward of economic stability pursuing its congressio-nally authorized dual mandate. It does not follow its own char-ter in the Federal Reserve Act (e.g., impermissibly buying cor-porate bonds). It does not operate based on economic theory or empirical data. It no longer pursues any identifiable public policy other than sheer political expediency. Fed governors do not follow "rules" or targets or models. They answer to no leg-islature or executive, except when cravenly collaborating with both to offload consequences onto future generations.

The Fed is, in effect, a lawless economic government unto itself. It serves as a bizarro-world *ad hoc* credit facility to the US financial sector, completely open ended, with no credit checks, no credit limits, no collateral requirements, no inter-est payments, and in some cases no repayments at all. It is the lender of first resort, a kind of reverse pawnshop which pays top dollar for rapidly declining assets. The Fed is now the Infi-nite Bank. It is run by televangelists, not bankers, and operates on faith.

That faith will be sorely tested.

Understanding the Current Crisis

1

Financialization: Why the Financial Sector Now Rules the Global Economy

by Ryan McMaken

To read or watch the news in today's world is to be confronted with a wide array of stories about financial organization and financial institutions. News about central banks, interest rates, and debt appear to be everywhere.

But it was not always the case that the financial sector and financial institutions were considered so important. Public policy in general was not always designed with a focus toward propping up banks, keeping interest rates low, and ensuring an ever greater flow of cheap and easy loans. Reporting on the minutiae of central banks—with the assumption that these changes directly impact nearly every facet of our lives—wasn't always the norm.

But that is where we are now.

The change is real and it's a thing called "financialization." It has arisen from of an economy that is increasingly focused on the financial sector at the expense of other areas of the economy. And it's relatively new. Scholars have suggested many causes for financialization, but they often end up just blaming markets. In fact, the true cause is decades of government and

Ryan McMaken, "Why the Financial Sector Now Rules the Global Economy," *Mises Wire* (March 18, 2020).

central bank policy devoted to inflating asset prices in financial markets and bailing out the financial sector again and again.

What Is Financialization?

"Financialization" is a term used to describe the process by which financial institutions like banks and hedge funds have taken over economies and political systems in much of the world.

Economist Gerald Epstein provides one definition: "the increasing importance of financial markets, financial motives, financial institutions, and financial elites in the operation of the economy and its governing institutions."[1]

Sociologist Greta Krippner provides another: "the tendency for profit making in the economy to occur increasingly through financial channels rather than through productive activities."[2]

Some scholars have attempted to measure financialization's prevalence in the United States. Carmen Dorobăț writes:

[1]Gerald Epstein, "Financialization, Rentier Interests, and Central Bank Policy," paper presented at the Political Economy Research Institute's Conference on "Financialization of the World Economy," December 7–8, 2001, University of Massachusetts, Amherst, Amherst, MA.

[2]Krippner is careful to clarify that by "productive" she means "the range of activities involved in the production or trade of commodities." Financial activities are, of course, not "necessarily *unproductive*," since financial services can indeed be valuable and productive services for the people who procure them. Krippner concludes: "To suggest that the economy has become financialized is to claim that the balance between these two sets of activities has swung strongly toward finance, not that the financial economy has become entirely uncoupled from production." Greta Krippner, *Capitalizing on Crisis* (Cambridge, MA: Harvard University Press, 2011).

Lin and Tomaskovic-Devey (2013) argue…one important tendency of the last decades has been the increased
participation of both financial and non-financial firms
in financial markets.

The two authors analyze the ratio between the financial
income (sum of interest, dividends, and capital gains)
and profits for manufacturing as well as all non-financial firms in the United States….They discover that
between 1970 and 2007, US firms have become more
and more financially driven, obtaining an increasingly
smaller share of their income from the sale of goods and
services, and about four times as much revenues from
financial activities compared to 1970.

Perhaps the most commonly given example of financialization is the expansion of the financial arms of US automobile
manufacturers:

General Motors established its financial arm General
Motors Acceptance Corporation (GMAC) in 1919 and
Ford established its financial service provider Ford
Motor Credit in 1959. Before the 1980s, the main function of these financial institutions was to provide their
automotive customers access to credit to increase car
sales. Starting in the 1980s, these firms broadened their
portfolio. GMAC entered mortgage lending in 1985.
In the same year, Ford purchased First Nationwide
Financial Corporation, the first thrift that operated at
the national level, to enter the savings and residential
loan markets. In the 1990s both GMAC and Ford Motor
Credit expanded their services to include insurance,
banking, and commercial finance.

By the early 2000s, a majority of GM's profits were coming
from its financial operations and not from automobile produc-

tion, and the S&P 500 was increasingly dominated by financial firms.[3]

What Is the Time Frame?

Historians of financialization typically place its origins in the late 1970s or during the 1980s. Sociologist Frank Dobbin, for example, concludes,

> We saw a rapid shift in the core business of the United States, from manufacturing not to service so much as to finance *per se*. As Simon Johnson pointed out, when the market peaked in 2001, finance accounted for 40% of profits in the American economy.

An oft-cited study by Lin and Tomaskovic-Devey shows that the "ratio of financial income to profits" more than dou-

---

[3]Moreover, as Gretchen Morgenson of the *New York Times* noted in the early 2000s:

> in recent years, financial services companies have quietly come to dominate the S&P 500.
>
> Right now, these companies make up 20.4 percent of the index, up from 12.8 percent 10 years ago. The current weight of financial services is almost double that of industrial company stocks and more than triple that of energy shares.
>
> …It is also worth noting that the current weight of financial services companies in the S&P is significantly understated because the 82 financial stocks in the index do not include General Electric, General Motors or Ford Motor. All of these companies have big financial operations that have contributed significantly to their earnings in recent years.

Gretchen Morgenson, "What Lurks Inside Your Index Fund," *New York Times* (website), June 20, 2004, http://www.nytimes.com/2004/06/20/business/yourmoney/20watch.html.

bled during the 1980s and then accelerated further during the 1990s.

Krippner notes:

An increasing trend indicates a higher share of revenues coming from financial relative to non-financial sources of income....The ratio is remarkably stable in the 1950s and 1960s, but begins to climb upward in the 1970s and then increases sharply over the course of the 1980s. In the late 1980s, the ratio peaks at a level that is approximately five times the levels typical of the immediate post-war decades.

Nor was this trend specific to the United States. The comparative data shows that most wealthy countries underwent similar transformations. According to Dobbin:

It happened in liberal market economies and coordinated market economies. It happened in economies with strong welfare states and weak welfare states. It happened in places where neoliberals took power early and places where neoliberals never quite ran the show. It happened regardless of the partisan coloration of government. And so on. The comparative data also give us something quite close to a natural experiment. There was one rich democratic country that escaped the fiscal crisis of the state in this period by the lucky expedient of discovering oil. That country was Norway. And— apart from the banking enclaves of Switzerland and Luxembourg, which did not financialize only because they were already so dependent on finance—Norway appears to be the only rich democratic country that did not undergo financialization in this period.[4]

[4]Frank Dobbin, "Review of Greta Krippner, *Capitalizing on Crisis: The Political Origins of the Rise of Finance*," *Trajectories* 23, no. 2 (2012): 2–4.

What Are Anticapitalists Saying Causes Financialization?

The causes of financialization have long been debated. Some causes suggested by scholars are economics based, and some are sociological and cultural.

Financialization as Endemic to Late-Stage Capitalism

In many cases, the charge that financialization is part of the natural evolution of markets has its roots in Marxism. Some authors have claimed that financialization is a cyclical process going back to the earliest days of capitalism, as described, for example, by Giovanni Arrighi in his book *The Long Twentieth Century*. According to Arrighi, capitalist systems begin with a productive phase, but end up, through increasingly intense global competition, moving into the financial sector in attempts to augment profits through financial speculation rather than through production. In this view, financialization is just another phase of development in a capitalist system and is baked into the market economy itself.

In this allegedly natural progression of capitalism, Arrighi states, "material expansions eventually lead to an over-accumulation of capital...and increasingly, competition turns from a positive-sum into a zero-sum (or even a negative-sum) game."[5]

In an earlier, less competitive age, owners of capital might have been motivated to invest most of it in physical plants, employment, and production. But globalization and "cut-throat competition" strengthen "the disposition of capitalist agencies to keep in liquid form a growing proportion of their

---

[5]Giovanni Arrighi, *The Long Twentieth Century: Money, Power, and the Origins of Our Times* (London, Verso Publishers, 2010), p. 372.

incoming cash flow."[6] This leads to competition among states for the capital that increasingly is accumulating in financial markets. The resulting political bias in favor of capital owners leads to "redistributions of income from all kinds of communities to the agencies that control mobile capital, thereby inflating and sustaining the profitability of financial deals largely divorced from trade and production."[7]

The Rise of the "Shareholder Value" Movement

A second proposed cause of financialization is the acceleration of the "shareholder value" movement. This theory, perhaps described in most detail by sociologist Gerald Davis, holds that prior to the 1970s publicly traded corporations were important social institutions that served several functions beyond just producing goods and services. Thanks to reforms imposed on them by Progressives, these corporations provided long-term employment and acted as catalysts for saving through their pension programs. According to Davis, "the public corporation became the central indispensable actor in the US economy."[8]

But this stabilizing *status quo*, Davis asserts, was destroyed by "bust-up takeovers" in the 1980s, and corporations were "split up into their constituent parts."[9] This led to substantial layoffs, and the corporate economy became less concentrated. Faced with new competition, corporations abandoned their previous social role and concentrated instead on shareholder value. This new corporate landscape was one in which shareholders frequently bought and sold their stock and corporations were forced to compete more fiercely to provide larger

[6]Ibid., p. 372.
[7]Ibid., p. 373.
[8]Gerald F. Davis, "After the Corporation," *Politics and Society* 41, no. 2: 283–30.
[9]Ibid., p. 287.

dividends and stock price growth. This sucked wealth out of pension funds and health programs, and it diminished the social benefits once provided by the old legacy corporations.

Consequently, financialization increased as investors and business owners increasingly adopted the idea that the sole purpose of a company is to increase shareholder value rather than production and market share. Although skillful production and growing market share can contribute to shareholder value, other methods could prove easier. Companies could increase their own shareholder value by growing their portfolios or by harnessing the power of a speculative frenzy. In any case, production of nonfinancial products and services took a back seat.

Or so the story goes.

Speculative Manias

A third theory states that speculative manias have over time fostered market demand for ever larger numbers of financial instruments that allow investors to make bets on nearly everything under the sun. These manias can be triggered by any number of causes, ranging from a bumper crop to the end of a war or the introduction of a new technology. These manias are then accelerated by cultural or psychological changes that accompany the perception that there is a "new reality." Economists have long attempted to use these cultural factors to explain economic events. John Maynard Keynes, for example, used the term "animal spirits" to summarize these nontangible changes.

These theories were popularized in part by economists Hyman Minsky and Charles Kindleberger, who held that once markets meet some levels of success, they have a tendency to drive overconfidence in financial markets for future investments.

Although the theory acknowledges that manias can be set off by outside factors, it nonetheless holds that markets *themselves* foster a tendency toward unrealistic expectations that "quickly become divorced from intrinsic values."[10]

According to Krippner, these "bubble theories view *processes internal to markets* as destabilizing rather than stabilizing to markets" (emphasis added).[11]

In any case, the result is that investors seek to reap greater financial rewards by betting on bubbles rather than through the production of physical goods and nonfinancial services. Financialization results.

Deregulation

"Deregulation" is also a prominent theme in many analyses of financialization.

Krippner, for example, concludes that "the turn to finance [was] set in motion by domestic financial deregulation in the 1970s."[12] This was followed by the loosening of many regulations on how banks paid out interest to depositors (also known as the pre-1986 version of Regulation Q).

In short, the abolition of various regulations on the financial sector—many of which had existed since the New Deal—set in motion a greater flow of capital and has led to more competition among banks and financial firms for the dollars of middle- and upper-class savers. Whereas the game of saving and investment had been relatively boring and sedate before the deregulation of the 1970s and '80s, the new competition that it unleashed led to a wide array of riskier—but potentially more rewarding—investment instruments.

---

[10]Krippner, *Capitalizing on Crisis*, p. 5.
[11]Ibid., p. 5.
[12]Ibid., p. 86.

In this narrative, money poured into the financial sector, since investment firms and banks were competing more than ever and driving up returns for investments. This sucked money out of other sectors which were still only offering the sorts of moderate, unfrenzied, and long-term returns that came with investing in manufacturing and nonfinancial services.

The Real Cause: Bailouts, Central Banks, and the "Greenspan Put"

The critics of financialization are correct that it exists. And they are sometimes correct in describing how events such as deregulation and manias have shaped the way financialization has occurred. But these theories fail to explain the *root causes* of how the financial sector came to be seen as a safe and profitable haven for so much capital.

The failure to identify the root cause has many implications for policy. After all, if it is assumed that markets themselves contain the seeds of financialization, and that these processes are merely unleashed when governments allow them greater freedom, then we easily conclude that markets cannot function without a sizable load of government regulation and that they are to blame for the various crises and panics of recent decades.

If markets repeatedly cause global crises, perhaps the market really is, to use David Stockman's term, "a doomsday machine."

But this narrative ignores key characteristics of the modern economy: namely that governments use fiscal and monetary policy to greatly weaken the discipline of the market. Governments do this through bailouts and through central banks' policies, designed to force down interest rates and increase the money supply.

These policies tend to be geared most toward the financial sector, so the risk of investing in financial sector institutions is reduced for those who hope to benefit from (full or partial) bailouts and easy borrowing in case of crisis. As "lenders of last resort," central banks are able to push liquidity to the financial sector with ease. This encourages investors to engage in higher-risk activities than they would in the absence of the knowledge that bailouts are likely in case of crisis.

Even those who think that markets themselves are geared toward encouraging excessive risk the problem of bailouts is apparent. For example, although Minsky and Kindleberger contended that speculative manias have their roots in markets, they nonetheless admitted that these manias often were made far worse by the presence of a central bank acting as a lender of last resort. As Krippner summarizes this point: "if financial institutions know that they will be bailed out, they are encouraged to speculate with abandon, making the crisis more severe when it finally comes."[13]

Thus, although changes in policy during the 1970s and early '80s may have *contributed* to financialization, the *foundational* cause was the removal of risk from the marketplace through government bailouts. After all, in the wake of deregulation it quickly became apparent that the new financial environment was not always an easy way to riches: Continental Illinois became the largest failed bank in US history in 1984. The stock market crashed in 1987. Had markets been allowed to function, this *would* have been a signal to markets that risky investments come with a downside for the specific investors involved.

But investors didn't learn that lesson at all. Continental Illinois was bailed out when the US government essentially nationalized the bank, protecting its shareholders. After the

---

[13]Krippner, p. 6.

market crashed in 1987, the new Fed chairman Alan Greenspan "immediately flooded the banking system with new reserves, by having the Fed Open Market Committee (FOMC) buy massive quantities of government securities from the repo market."

In other words, this new post-1970s world of financialization was not even a decade old before federal policymakers started teaching investors that if they get into trouble federal policymakers will bail them out.[14]

By the early 1990s, the US had entered the world of the so-called "Greenspan Put," under which it quickly became clear that the central bank would intervene to rescue markets whenever investors took on too much risk. While financial sector institutions could reap the rewards of good times, they would be rescued by taxpayers when times turned bad. Under Greenspan, the central bank was there to bail the financial sector out repeatedly through various means. We witnessed this with the Mexican financial crisis, the Asian financial crisis of the late 1990s, and the bailouts that followed the Dot-com bust. Greenspan was at the center of inflating the housing bubble after 2004.

The Greenspan Put didn't go away after Greenspan retired from the Federal Reserve Board. It was continued in various forms by all his successors. So, it's easy to see why under these conditions the financial sector becomes the go-to place for investors relative to other sectors. Why invest in industries that won't be bailed out when excessive risk taking in the financial sector is likely to be rewarded for engaging in ever greater risks?

Even when dramatic and targeted bailouts are not the goal, repeated efforts by central banks to inject more liquidity into markets through new money creation has favored the

---

[14]Henry Liu, "The Unlearned Lesson of the 1987 Crash," Roosevelt Institute, 2010, https://rooseveltinstitute.org/unlearned-lesson-1987-crash/.

financial sector relative to other sectors of the economy. Robert Blumen has described the mechanisms that keep central bank policies that drive asset price inflation from showing up in consumer price inflation. This means that price increases in financial assets like stocks further inflate the perceived value of the financial sector relative to other sectors. All of this drives financialization well beyond what would occur in an unhampered market.

Financialization and Our Bubble Economy

Although researchers like Arrighi, Davis, and Krippner all describe various aspects of financialization, these theories don't work as satisfying explanations of the phenomenon. Even if cultural changes, new investment instruments, or a lack of government regulation allowed for new investment avenues in the financial sector, there is no reason to believe that the very real human fear of monetary loss has fundamentally changed. In a functioning market the promise of immense profit through investment in the financial sector is tempered by the fear of taking a loss. As investors see banks fail and stocks take a beating, they normally view these events for what they are: a demonstration of the downside of financialization.

But governments and central banks haven't allowed that to happen in recent decades.

So, it's not enough to attempt to describe financialization in terms of cultural changes or vague Marxian notions of capitalist evolution. At the heart of the issue is government intervention designed to provide the investor class with greater gains and fewer losses.

Yet the prevailing "wisdom" among policymakers and central bankers is that ever greater amounts of financialization—propped up by repeated government interventions —are somehow just a natural and inescapable feature of the market economy. With each new bubble and each new crisis, the central banks become ever more willing to try risky and "nontraditional" interventions, whether it's negative interest rates, the abolition of physical cash, or ever larger purchases of near-worthless assets. Thanks to decades of government-fueled financialization, the stakes climb ever higher.

But perhaps the most unfortunate part of it all is that as the crises mount, markets get the blame for what would never have happened had markets actually been allowed to function.

2

Are Central Banks Nationalizing the Economy?

by Daniel Lacalle

The *Financial Times* recently ran an article that states that "leading central banks now own a fifth of their governments' total debt."

The figures are staggering.

- Without any recession or crisis, major central banks are purchasing more than $200 billion a month in government and private debt, led by the ECB and the Bank of Japan.

- The Federal Reserve owns more than 14 percent of the US total public debt.

- The ECB and BOJ balance sheets exceed 35 percent and 70 percent of their GDP.

- The Bank of Japan is now a top ten shareholder in 90 percent of the Nikkei.

Daniel Lacalle, "Are Central Banks Nationalizing the Economy?" *Mises Wire* (August 24, 2017). Originally published at DLacalle.com.

- The ECB owns 9.2 percent of the European corporate bond market and more than 10 percent of the main European countries' total sovereign debt.

- The Bank of England owns between 25 percent and 30 percent of the UK's sovereign debt.

A recent report by Nick Smith, an analyst at CLSA, warns of what he calls "the nationalization of the secondary market."

The Bank of Japan, with its ultra-expansionary policy, which only expands its balance sheet, is on course to become the largest shareholder of the Nikkei 225's largest companies. In fact, the Japanese central bank already accounts for 60 percent of the ETFs market (Exchange traded funds) in Japan.

What can go wrong? Overall, the central bank not only generates greater imbalances and a poor result in a "zombified" economy as the extremely loose policies perpetuate imbalances, weaken money velocity, and incentivize debt and malinvestment.

Believing that this policy is harmless because "there is no inflation" and unemployment is low is dangerous. The government issues massive amounts of debt and cheap money promotes overcapacity and poor capital allocation. As such, productivity growth collapses, real wages fall and purchasing power of currencies fall, driving the real cost of living up and debt to grow more than real GDP. That is why, as we have shown in previous articles, total debt has soared to 325 percent of GDP while zombie companies reach crisis-high levels, according to the Bank of International Settlements.

Government-issued liabilities monetized by the central bank are not high-quality assets, they are an IOU that is transferred to the next generations, and it will be repaid in three ways: with massive inflation, with a series of financial crises, or with large unemployment. Currency purchasing power destruction is not a growth policy, it is stealing from future generations. The "placebo" effect of spending today the Net Present Value of those IOUs means that, as GDP, productivity and real disposable income do not improve, at least as much as the debt issued, we are creating a time bomb of economic imbalances that only grows and will explode sometime in the future. The fact that the evident ball of risk is delayed another year does not mean that it does not exist.

The government is not issuing "productive money" just a promise of higher revenues from higher taxes, higher prices or confiscation of wealth in the future. Money supply growth is a loan that government borrows but we, citizens, pay. The payment comes with the destruction of purchasing power and confiscation of wealth via devaluation and inflation. The "wealth effect" of stocks and bonds rising is inexistent for the vast majority of citizens, as more than 90 percent of average household wealth is in deposits.

In fact, massive monetization of debt is just a way of perpetuating and strengthening the crowding-out effect of the public sector over the private sector. It is a *de facto* nationalization. Because the central bank does not go "bankrupt," it just transfers its financial imbalances to private banks, businesses, and families.

The central bank can "print" all the money it wants and the government benefits from it, but the ones that suffer financial repression are the rest. By generating subsequent financial crises through loose monetary policies and always being the main beneficiary of the boom, and the bust, the public sector comes out from these crises more powerful and more indebted, while the private sector suffers the crowding-out effect in crisis times, and the taxation and wealth confiscation effect in expansion times.

No wonder that government spending to GDP is now almost 40 percent in the OECD and rising, the tax burden is at all-time highs and public debt soars.

Monetization is a perfect system to nationalize the economy passing all the risks of excess spending and imbalances to taxpayers. And it always ends badly. Because two plus two does not equal twenty-two. As we tax the productive to perpetuate and subsidize the unproductive, the impact on purchasing power and wealth destruction is exponential.

To believe that this time will be different and governments will spend all that massive "very expensive free money" wisely is simply delusional. The government has all the incentives to overspend as its goal is to maximize budget and increase bureaucracy as means of power. It also has all the incentives to blame its mistakes on an external enemy. Governments always blame someone else for their mistakes. Who lowers rates from 10% to 1%? Governments and central banks. Who is blamed for taking "excessive risk" when it explodes? You and me. Who increases money supply, demands "credit flow," and imposes financial repression because "savings are too high"? Governments and central banks. Who is blamed when it explodes? Banks for "reckless lending" and "de-regulation".

Of course, governments can print all the money they want, what they cannot do is convince you and me that it has a value, that the price and amount of money they impose is real just because the government says so. Hence lower real investment, and lower productivity. Citizens and companies are not crazy for not falling into the trap of low rates and high asset inflation. They are not amnesiac.

It is called financial repression for a reason, and citizens will always try to escape from theft.

What is the "hook" to let us buy into it? Stock markets rise, bonds fall, and we are led to believe that asset inflation is a reflection of economic strength.

Then, when the central bank policy stops working—either from lack of confidence or because it is simply part of the liquidity—and markets fall to their deserved valuations, many will say that it is the fault of "speculators," not the central speculator.

When it erupts, you can bet your bottom dollar that the consensus will blame markets, hedge funds, lack of regulation and not enough intervention. Perennial intervention mistakes are "solved" with more intervention. Government won on the way up, and wins on the way down. Like a casino, the house always wins.

Meanwhile, the famous structural reforms that had been promised disappear like bad memories.

It is a clever Machiavellian system to end free markets and disproportionately benefit governments through the most unfair of competitions: having unlimited access to money and credit and none of the risks. And passing the bill to everyone else.

If you think it does not work because the government does not do a lot more, you are simply dreaming.

3

The Menace of Sub-Zero Interest-Rate Policy

by Brendan Brown

Sub-zero interest rate policy as Europe and Japan have practiced for many years menaces global economic prosperity. Yet Congress and the White House are strangely silent on the issue; even a prophetic messenger would not arouse them.

Two monetary episodes—one historical and counterfactual, the other contemporary and real—highlight the nature of the danger.

First, history: throughout the heyday of the gold standard from the mid-1860s to 1914, short term money market rates in London rarely fell below 1–2 percent p.a. and then only briefly. Typically, these short rates were highly volatile day-to-day, but few cared.

The medium and long-term rates were much steadier, their level reflecting a massive amount of decentralized information in the market-place stemming from individual borrowing and lending decisions. Perceptions of the likely average short-term rate over the long-run set a floor to long-term rates (as speculators could borrow at the long rate and roll-over lending at the short).

Brendan Brown, "The Menace of Sub-Zero Interest-Rate Policy," *Mises Wire* (March 12, 2019).

Walter Bagehot famously observed that "John Bull can stand many things, but he cannot stand interest rates of 2 percent" (meaning lower rates would make him mad—in today's sense of irrational exuberance or desperate search for yield). The gold standard worked in a way which respected that wisdom.

If short-term rates fell towards zero, there would be a heavy "drain of gold" as the public converted deposits and notes into the yellow metal; a growing shortage of gold reserves (in the banking system) would force a tightening of monetary conditions. This mechanism depended on the natural scarcity of gold and its unique attractions. "High-powered money" under fiat money regimes has never enjoyed these properties.

The implicit floor to nominal interest rates was no barrier to the invisible hands achieving economic recovery from recession. This occurred in the context of stable prices in the very long run, not permanent inflation as preached by the architects and officials of today's 2 percent inflation standard. Crucially goods prices fell to a below-average level during the weak phase of the business cycle and were widely expected to rise back to normal or above in the expansion phase.

What do today's central bankers think of Bagehot's wisdom about John Bull?

They deny that asset inflation exists. And they would not request their research departments, filled up with neo-Keynesian economists, to conduct the following counterfactual analysis.

If central banks had all respected a 1–2 percent floor to interest rates through the last decade how would economic recovery have taken place and what would have been the nature of the expansion?

ECB Chief Draghi for one has never broached the topic of asset inflation. He has never had to answer a serious question on the topic at his tedious press conferences or hearings before the European Parliament. Even so the Chief has not been able to totally sidestep a public discussion which reveals indirectly some of the dangers of zero and negative rates in this present cycle. His fellow-officials have also commented.

The subject: a key difference between how the ECB on the one hand and the Bank of Japan (BoJ) plus the Swiss National Bank (SNB) on the other have been administering negative interest rate policy in this cycle.

The powerful bank lobby in Germany has been asking why the ECB does not copy the SNB and BoJ in only charging banks negative rates on a marginal slice of their deposits with the central bank rather than the entirety.

Chief Draghi has not provided a direct or frank answer but admits that the issue is "under review." His reticence hints at some of the disturbing motives behind negative rate policies.

In puzzling out why the ECB is administering negative rate policy in harsh fashion as regards the banks which are plush with reserves let's start by identifying what common purpose it could achieve with the BoJ and SNB by keeping to a lighter touch (imposing negative rates on only a small marginal slice of deposits placed with the central bank by its member banks).

This common aim is currency manipulation.

The national money (or union money in the case of the euro) depreciates as a flight of capital occurs out of negative rate assets. All are not equal in this flight. Banks seek to shelter their regular domestic clients from negative rates. They pass on the cost of the negative rate fee on their reserves only to wholesale and foreign depositors, also taking account of the squeezed rates of return obtainable on their other assets including loans and short-maturity government bonds.

In effect the negative rate regime operates partly like a system of exchange restrictions which imposes penalties on foreign inflows into the domestic money market.

German banks are more stressed in sheltering their depositors from negative rates than their Swiss and Japanese counterparts given the harsh treatment of the ECB. In consequence the shelter they offer is less broad and deep and bank shareholders have to pay more heavily for its provision via diminished profits.

Why doesn't Chief Draghi relent? Because that would mean less subsidy to Italian banks, stupid! The ECB takes advantage of the negative rate fee it charges on deposits (and German banks are the main net creditor of the euro-system reflecting the huge German savings surplus) to make subsidized loans most of all to Italian banks.

If ECB Chief Draghi were just pursuing currency manipulation, yes, he could please the German bank lobby (and the Bundesbank which pleads on their behalf). But he has this second purpose in mind. Hence the prevarication.

Ultimately these transfer consequences of negative rates within Europe (mainly from Germany to Italy) are not a matter for anyone else, including the Trump Administration. German voters should have their say. The aspect of concern for the US is currency manipulation.

The most direct remedy would be for the US Treasury to add negative and zero rate policy to its list of tests as to whether a foreign government is pursuing currency manipulation. Further the US could use its considerable influence at the IMF, notwithstanding its French managing director, to make negative and zero rate policy a suspect activity inconsistent with the goal of stamping out beggar-your-neighbor policy.

There is absolutely no likelihood of the Trump administration taking either step. For banning negative rates in Japan and Europe could precipitate the passage of present asset inflation into its final phase of crisis ahead of the 2020 elections. Much better to concentrate on direct action to reduce the ill-effects on US trade of currency manipulation.

4

Central Bank's Crusade Against Risk

by Thorsten Polleit

Since the latest the crisis in 2008/2009, central banks around the world have been doing their best to expel risks from financial markets. By lowering interest rates, fixing them at extremely low levels, or issuing more credit and money, monetary policymakers make sure that ailing borrowers are kept afloat. In fact, central banks have put a "safety net" under the economies and the financial markets in particular. As it seems, this measure has been working quite effectively over the last ten years or so.

Investors do no longer fear that big borrowers—be it big governments or big banks and big corporates—could default, as evidenced by the low credit spread environment. Liquidity in basically all important credit market segments is high, and borrowers experience no trouble rolling over their maturing debt. What is more, stock market valuations have continued to increase, significantly propped up by central banks' easy monetary policy. For low interest rates help drive stock prices and their valuation levels up.

Thorsten Polleit, "Central Bank's Crusade Against Risk," *Mises Wire* (May 15, 2019).

Artificially suppressed interest rates lead to higher present values of firms' discounted future profits. Furthermore, the decline in credit costs tends to increase corporate profits, thereby also boosting stock prices and their valuations. By no means less important, the low interest rate regime has caused firms' capital costs to go down, encouraging additional investment activity, which is stoking investor optimism and feeding a buoyant stock market.

Decline in risk perception, rising stock valuation
Financial market stress indicator and price-earnings ratio of US stock market[1]

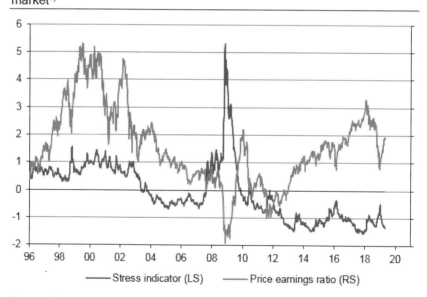

Source: Thomson Financial; graphic by Degussa.

As a measure of risk perception, figure 1 shows a "financial market stress indicator", together with the price-earnings ratio of the US stock market. From eyeballing the series, one can easily see that, since around 2009, the PE ratio has been rising considerably, while risk perception, as measured by the financial market stress indicator, has gone down substantially and has been hovering at relatively low levels since around the middle of 2014. The message of the chart is, therefore: Risk down, stock valuations up.

Of course, there is nothing wrong with this development per se, were it not for the fact that the decline in risk perception does not come naturally, but has been orchestrated by central banks' many interventions in the credit and financial system. In particular, by artificially lowering market interest rates, central banks have triggered a "boom", which produces pretty-to-look-at official data (on GDP, investment, employment, and such), but which is, and unfortunately so, built on quicksand.

The boom will only continue if and when market interest rates remain at suppressed levels, or are lowered even further. For if interest rates were to rise, various investments would turn out to be unprofitable; loans would default; banks would run up losses and rein in their credit supply; unemployment would rise; and so on. In other words: Higher interest rates would turn the boom into bust, for they would actually collapse the production and employment structure that has been nurtured by a policy of extremely low interest rates.

This is why central banks are most likely to continue with their "crusade against risk." That is, they will very likely keep their interest rates at current low levels for a very long time or will, where it is still possible, lower them even further. For how long can this go on? Presumably no one knows for sure. At least on a scientific basis it is impossible to forecast when the crisis will hit, when the current boom will turn into bust. It might be a bitter pill to swallow, but it goes well beyond the science of economics to make any such predictions.

In view of central banks having effectively taken full control of the credit market, however, the odds are now that the boom will go on longer than many observers presumably suspect. For if central banks succeed in keeping a lid on market interest rates, a very important correction mechanism that could potentially turn the boom into bust—and that is a return of market interest rates to "normal levels"—is effectively switched off; central banks' crusade against risk proves to be devilishly efficacious indeed.

To be sure: By putting to rest investor risk concerns—in the form of, say, credit default, liquidity, reinvestment and horizon risks—central banks exert enormously distorting effects—which come clearly on top of the distortions resulting from a lowering of central banks' key interest rates. Not only financial assets get increasingly mis-priced. Capital goods and all kinds of commodity prices get also heavily distorted (as these goods are priced according to their discounted marginal value product).

If central banks get away with their current monetary policies, then the probably greatest economic and financial distortion the world has ever seen will be fabricated: malinvestment, price bubbles and over-leveraging on a truly epic scale, accompanied by a dwindling purchasing power of the currencies involved. A plausible near-term scenario: For major central banks around the globe have teamed up in an effort to keep the current boom going, and there should be little doubt that they will do whatever it takes to do just that.

The extreme downside scenario, if and when it kicks in, is no doubt very unpleasant. In the words of Ludwig von Mises (1881–1973), it is this:

> There is no means of avoiding the final collapse of a boom brought about by credit expansion. The alternative is only whether the crisis should come sooner as a result of a voluntary abandonment of further credit expansion, or later as a final and total catastrophe of the currency system involved.[1]

---

[1]Ludwig von Mises, *Human Action* (Auburn, Ala.: Mises Institute, 1998), p. 570.

Fortunately, man's future is not foreordained, as Marxian dialectic materialism wants people make to believe. On the contrary. Mans' ideas and actions shape his future; fatalism is logically incompatible with his nature. Having said that, we have good reason to take side with Hans F. Sennholz (1922–2007), who noted: "[W]e are ever hopeful that, in the end, reason and virtue will prevail over error and evil."[2] It is by no means an oversimplification to say here that the monetary problem in this world can be solved quite easily.

The key step would be opening up a free market for money: that is allowing for a system to emerge in which people can freely decide which kind of money they wish to use. People would then no longer be effectively forced to use central banks' monopolized currencies, and central banks could no longer abuse the monopoly power for catering to the needs of, say, the deep state and big business, which of course comes at the expense of the majority of the people.

A free market in money would also have the potential to mitigate the severity of the economic, financial and social crisis the current monetary system holds in store for basically all of us.

---

[2]Hans F. Sennholz, *Age of Inflation* (1979), p. 178.

5

The Ghosts of Failed Banks Have Returned

by Alasdair Macleod

Recently, something unusual happened: instead of the more normal reverse repurchase agreements, the Fed escalated its repurchase agreements (repos).

For the avoidance of doubt, a reverse repo by the Fed involves the Fed borrowing money from commercial banks, secured by collateral held on its balance sheet, typically US Treasury bills. Reverse repos withdraw liquidity from the banking system. With a repo, the opposite happens: the Fed takes in collateral from the banking system and lends money against the collateral, injecting liquidity into the system. The use of reverse repos can be regarded as the Fed's principal liquidity management tool when the banks have substantial reserves parked with the Fed, which is the case today.

Having inflated its balance sheet following the Lehman crisis by buying US Treasury bonds—thereby increasing bank reserves—from 2011 the Fed started to increase its reverse repo position until 2017. In other words, it was taking liquidity

Alasdair Macleod, "The Ghosts of Failed Banks Have Returned," *Mises Wire* (October 11, 2019).

out of the banking system, having previously injected massive amounts of it by means of quantitative easing following the Lehman crisis. From early-2017 to October 2018, outstanding reverse repos then halved, implying liquidity was being added. Since then they have increased by roughly half to $325bn, reducing liquidity.[1]

What spooked market commentators was the unexpected increase in the repo rate, which on Tuesday 17 September suddenly jumped from the previous Friday's level of 2.19 percent to as much as 10 percent. By escalating its repo position, a targeted liquidity injection from the Fed followed as it struggled to maintain control over the repo rate, taking its outstanding repos from less than $20bn to $53bn. The Fed cut its Fed Funds Rate to a target of 1.75–2.0 percent the following day.

On Wednesday, 18 September the Fed's repo position increased again from $53bn to $75 bn. Furthermore, on Thursday and Friday respectively the Fed's repo position remained elevated, reaching $105bn last Monday. Interestingly, overnight dollar Libor declined slightly, in line with the reduction in the Fed Funds Rate, apparently unaffected by the higher repo rates in the US, confirming it is specifically a US problem involving the large banks.

There have been a number of explanations by expert commentators as to why the repo rate rocketed, none of them satisfactory. It reminds one of verse 29 of Fitzgerald's *Rubaiyat of Omar Khayyam*:

Myself when young did eagerly frequent
Doctor and Saint, and heard great Argument
About it and about; but evermore
Came out by the same Door as in I went.

---

[1]See Federal Reserve Statistical Release H.4.1, Factors Affecting Reserve Balances for the latest information on both repos and reverse repos.

Instead, I have a strong suspicion we are seeing the ghosts of past bank failures, most recently in the UK, the sorry tale of Northern Rock which I closely observed. For non-British readers, a short reminder: as a licensed bank, Northern Rock was a mortgage lender which got into difficulties in September 2007, before being nationalized the following February. An old-fashioned run with customers queuing outside its branches seeking to withdraw their deposits had alerted the general public to Northern Rock's problems. It was unable to tap wholesale money markets, because other banks were unwilling to lend to it on an uncollateralized basis.

The establishment missed the point. As Gillian Tett wrote in the *Financial Times* at the time, there were increasing concerns over how Libor was operating. There was a growing divergence in the rates that different banks were quoting in the various currencies priced in Libor, discriminating against the smaller borrowers (actually, an indication of growing counterparty risk, not a supposed failure of Libor). Furthermore, larger banks were reducing their exposure to Libor by sourcing funds from the treasury operations of large companies and using the developing repo market (which is collateralized, unlike Libor—a further indication of increasing systemic concerns) to maintain their overnight balances instead.

I recall vividly being in RP Martin's office (then a leading money broker—now part of BGC Partners) in December that year, when all Libor offers mysteriously disappeared, leaving borrowers stranded. Having expected for some time that the credit bubble would come to a head and burst, I took this to be a significant signal of a developing crisis.

The following February, Northern Rock, which had depended on money markets for its financing, collapsed and was nationalized by the government, and the great financial crisis duly followed.

Could the erringly similar repo failure today be the ghost of Northern Rock returning to haunt us in New York? If so, we now have a far larger credit bubble to pop, and the figures in the repo market are in tens of billions, instead of tens of millions. This time it is perhaps less obvious to the general public, because old-fashioned public bank runs are probably a thing of the past.

The crisis brewing in 2007 was attributed to residential property and liar loans in America, securitized into collateralized debt obligations (CDOs), sliced and diced to give the appearance of tranches riskless to investors, while the risk was pushed into smaller equity and mezzanine tranches, retained by the sponsors. If we have a repeat performance of that, it is likely to involve the successor to CDOs, collateralized loan obligations (CLOs). They do roughly the same thing, but with low quality corporate debt.

This is why we must take notice of trouble in the repo market, and not dismiss it as just a one-off. The reason for its failure has little to do with, as some commentators have suggested, a general liquidity shortage. That argument is challenged by the increase in the Fed's reverse repos from $230bn in October 2018 to $325bn on 18 September, which would not have been implemented if there was a general shortage of liquidity. Rather, it appears to be a systemic problem; another Northern Rock, but far larger. Today we call such an event a black swan.

What is Today's Northern Rock—or is it a Credit-Anstalt?

We cannot dismiss the possibility that a large non-American bank operating through a US-licensed subsidiary is perceived by its peers as too risky as a counterparty. This being the case, the most likely candidate is Deutsche Bank, which may be needing a significant liquidity replacement for fleeing deposits, having just concluded the sale of its prime brokerage to BNP. It is one thing to remove a business from the asset side of a bank's balance sheet, but another to secure the far larger deposits that go with it.

Last July, Bloomberg reported that when the BNP deal was first mooted, Deutsche Bank clients were pulling out a billion dollars every day. Presumably, that was manageable, with enough liquidity on the asset side of Deutsche Bank's very large balance sheet to iron out any difficulties, and it had its access to the US repo market.

Coinciding with current events, the BNP deal was finally signed and announced only last Monday, though it would have been known in New York banking circles last week when the difficulties in the repo market surfaced. Furthermore, large depositors would have almost certainly been made aware of the timing in advance in an effort to keep them onside, and some of them may have chosen to simply withdraw their deposits.

The sums involved could easily be large enough to marry up with the support provided by the Fed through the increased level of its repo exposure. Furthermore, we cannot dismiss the likelihood of the problem spreading to the US primary dealers of other foreign banks, including BNP itself.

For comparison, the time-lapse between the failure of the Libor market and Northern Rock's nationalisation was less than two months. We cannot know for certain whether the trouble in the American repo market and the obvious difficulties faced by Deutsche Bank are definitely linked, let alone comparable in terms of time and outcome to the Northern Rock experience. But banks, hedge funds and operators of synthetic ETFs will be watching closely.

Synthetic ETFs are comprised of cash, near cash and bonds (which are meant to be liquid but often not), while matching their price performance to an index through derivatives. Having grown to an estimated $4 trillion overall, through synthetic

ETFs the industry has accumulated substantial quantities of cash, bank deposits and near-cash at large banks with primary dealerships.

If the repo troubles escalate, there is a danger the investment management industry will start to move these funds from banks perceived to have increasing counterparty and operational risk, with potentially devastating consequences for all involved. Cynics have thought for a long time that the ETF industry would end in disaster for investors, without having a convincing explanation of how it would happen. Perhaps we are now beginning to see early evidence pointing to the ending of the ETF phenomenon, and to therefore be able to anticipate the knock-on effects on financial and derivative markets generally.

Returning to the subject of bank relationships, a more worrying comparison between Deutsche Bank and the Northern Rock episode could be with the Credit-Anstalt crisis of May 1931. It was the largest bank in Austria, just as Deutsche is the largest in Germany, a far larger country with a more important economy. Then in Austria and today in Germany, European economies were tipping into recession, forcing large losses onto their banks. Following the 1931 crisis, within months not only Austria but other European countries endured financial distress, the gold exchange standard began to disintegrate, and the international flow of goods was disrupted by growing protectionism as governments tried to batten down the hatches.

The flight of foreign creditors triggered by these events rapidly turned a major crisis in a minor country into a major crisis for all Europe and beyond. Today, if the same fate were to happen to Deutsche Bank, not only would it be on a far larger scale, but there is the additional question of the gross notional value of its derivatives book of nearly $50 trillion and the future of the euro itself. Is it any wonder, if Deutsche is indeed at the centre of last week's repo crisis, that other major banks, have decided to step back and refused to accept its collateral in a repo?

The other major banks appear to have left the Fed to pick up the pieces by taking over the repo market. Another potential problem is China, with the Financial Times reporting only eleven days ago that Chinese groups are shedding $40bn in global assets, with a sub-heading that warned US divestments are soaring.[2] Then there is the unexpected escalation of domestic funding requirements faced by Saudi Arabia in the wake of the attack on her oil refining facilities, almost certainly being covered by the sale of dollar balances in New York.

This confirms that some of the liquidity problems exposed by the repo market may be due to a reduction in dollar balances by both foreign corporations and governments, contrary to a wide-held belief that in a crisis, foreigners should be scrambling to buy dollars. It could throw an unexpected spotlight on US banks, including those with foreign ownership, with direct and indirect Chinese and Saudi connections. Though as mentioned below, with $307.9bn withdrawn in the year to July, foreign withdrawals appear to be a more widespread problem than exposed by current events. Whether it is the major force behind the repo crisis should be considered in the light of the dollar's performance on the foreign exchanges, which has been remarkably steady in recent weeks.

Collateralized and Leveraged Loans May Be to Follow

The course of a credit crisis often starts with an initial shock followed by the uncovering of deeper problems. Almost everyone is taken by surprise by the initial shock, not realising its

---

[2]*Financial Times*, "Chinese groups turn seller to shed $40bn in global assets."

importance as a signal for a change in bankers' attitudes to risk. The expression of purely technical reasons for the disruption in the repo market assume that what was known before still applies and there are no other factors involved; just an error of judgement by the authorities in managing markets. This is likely to be a mistake because markets are dynamic, and we can identify three separate reasons why no one should be complacent:

1. A slowdown in the US economy, yet to be reflected in backward-looking statistics, leads to a reduction in corporate cash levels and a drawdown of revolving credit to finance accumulating inventory. US banks may be already seeing evidence of this in some sectors.

2. There has been a reduction in dollar balances by foreign corporations and governments held through correspondent banks (note that in the twelve months to July 2019, there have been net withdrawals of $307.9bn[3]). Bankers will have been assuming that this is a temporary phenomenon, given the dollar's reserve status. That hope is now being dispelled.

3. American banks are becoming more cautious of counterparty risk in wholesale money markets generally.

Following the current repo hiatus, a combination of all three is likely to lead to a change in the thinking of commercial bankers, with the first two fueling the third. As to whether the problem is regarded as temporary or rings serious alarm bells, we need to dig more deeply into the marginal loan busi-

---

[3]See Line 29 in the table at U.S. Department of the Treasury Press Release "Treasury International Capital Data for July."

ness which could tip the banks into a collective crisis, even if the immediate repo problem subsides. An obvious candidate is CLOs and uncollateralized leveraged loans.

According to the Bank for International Settlements, outstanding collateralized loan obligations are split with approximately $1.2 trillion in US dollars, and $200bn equivalent in euros.[4] The dollar exposure accounts for half of all leveraged loans in the US financial system, so the total size of the US leveraged loan market is more like $2.4 trillion, which compares with the book value of total equity capital for commercial banks in the US of $1.95 trillion. While direct bank exposure to CLOs is estimated at only $250bn, they are bound to have the lion's share of the rest of the leveraged loan market, giving them a total exposure of up to $1.5 trillion without indirect exposure being taken into account. Most of American banks' equity capital is therefore at risk.

Collateralized or not, leveraged loans are bank loans to highly indebted corporations with high interest servicing costs barely covered by earnings, and mostly rated at less than investment grade. In an economic downturn these are the businesses that are the first to fail, and underlying asset quality is already reported by the BIS to be deteriorating. Furthermore, as global interest rates and bond yields have fallen towards and into negative territory, the demand for higher yielding CLOs has increased and the underlying quality decreased. The debt to earnings ratio of leveraged borrowers securitised in CLOs has risen and CLOs without maintenance covenants have grown from 20 percent in 2012 to 80 percent in 2018.

In its report, the BIS warns that there are additional spillovers that could arise from disruptions in market liquidity, a statement that is particularly apt considering the current dis-

---

[4]See *BIS Quarterly Review, International,* "International banking and financial market developments" (September 2019): 11–14.

ruption in the repo market. Given the involvement of hedge funds, fixed income mutual funds and bank loan funds, when the credit cycle has more obviously turned there will almost certainly be a rush to sell these CLOs, likely to lead to fire sales with a potential to cascade losses in the manner seen with residential property CDOs eleven years ago.

Consider, for a moment, the position of a typical large US bank and the changing commercial motivations of its directors. Following the Lehman crisis, lending margins to non-financial corporations never really compensated for the risk of extending credit to anything other than large corporations and consumers prepared to pay credit card rates of interest. As the economy gradually recovered, loans to investment grade borrowers increased. Along with higher yields and with a AAA rating attached, lending to sub-investment grade borrowers became increasingly available through CLOs. Once the CLO ice was broken, even better yields were available by lending directly to sub-investment grade borrowers, the key being improving economic prospects underpinning the borrowers' earnings. Furthermore, the bank's competitors were also allocating increasing amounts of credit towards borrowers of this sort, so it is nearly impossible for our typical large bank not to follow them.

So far, all lending will appear to conform to the bank's lending risk criteria, assuming of course that economic prospects are improving. The moment that stops, the directors of the bank will feel exposed and try to contain, then reduce their exposure to loan risk. In this respect, the change in the Fed's interest rate policy is the clearest signal of an economic slowdown and rings the bell on the soundness of lending assumptions. This also includes considerations of systemic risk, in other words the risk of lending money to other banks and financial institutions deemed to be exposed to both CLOs and other leveraged loans.

As with all humanity, the rapid transposition from greed to fear afflicts bankers as well. If anything, given their tight group-thinking it is especially acute, turning on a dime. The expectation that the Fed was going to cut its Fed Funds Rate could act as a catalyst for fear, instead of laying concerns to rest over lending margin prospects. And bankers have good reason to be extremely concerned when they cast their attention towards geopolitics, the global and domestic economic outlook, and the growing threat of negative interest rates. And here, the news is not encouraging.

Geopolitics and the Destruction of Global Trade

When President Trump embarked on a policy of penalizing China with tariffs, the general assumption in financial markets was that a settlement would be achieved before long. Instead, the situation has deteriorated and realistically is nowhere nearer resolution. The effect of the trade dispute has been not only to harm both parties but has resulted in collateral damage as well.

Germany, whose fastest growing market was China, has been driven into recession, with last Monday's purchasing managers' index headlined as "simply awful". With Germany being the locomotive pulling along all the other Eurozone members, this is already leading to deepening concerns for the Eurozone's outlook and a resumption of asset purchases by the ECB (quantitative easing) is now due in November. It is also very bad news for Germany's hard-pressed banking community, represented in New York by Deutsche Bank.

US banks will undoubtedly be increasingly aware of the negative impact of Trump's tariffs on international trade through the credit demands of their customers. Now they see America drifting towards a new conflict in the Middle East against Iran. Saudi's oil production has been hit by drones and missiles, allegedly from Iran, and the oil price could well increase substantially as a result. It could even drag Russia and China into a conflict. Hong Kong has been paralyzed by riots, with China suspecting American provocation.

Clearly, the conflict between America and China has escalated well beyond just tariffs, making it difficult to visualize how the damage to global trade can be corrected. The economic outlook is therefore set to deteriorate further, with no end to it in sight. From a banker's viewpoint, a global recession is the greatest threat to his business as a financial intermediary between failing borrowers and nervous depositors. He can only survive by taking anticipatory action to avoid potential losses.

Some bankers will have been clinging to the hope that the Fed, by reducing interest rates and if necessary, reintroducing quantitative easing, will rescue the US economy from outright recession and that economic growth will resume. Without doubt, this is the advice being given to management by in-house economists, unfamiliar with today's destructive dynamics of tariffs combining with a failing late-stage credit cycle. These conditions were last seen in 1929, when Smoot-Hawley tariffs coincided with the end of a long phase of credit expansion. However, there is little statistical evidence so far that the US economy faces anything more than a pause in economic growth, which is why stock prices and other collateralized assets have held their values.

The reality is that a credit crisis cannot be avoided, only deferred. It is also hard to see how zero interest rates reduced from current levels can be enough to rescue markets that, on the evidence from the repo market, are beginning to price growing counterparty risk into interbank loans. Recent experience and central banking models suggest that dollar interest rates should be reduced by at least four or five percent to stabilize the situation, putting them deep into negative territory.

And as for negative rates, there is no development more likely to drive depositors into gold, silver and other media to escape from the taxation of negative rates on deposits.

Outcomes and Their Timing

Having been warned that not all is hunky-dory in Repo-land, the more forward-thinking bankers will begin to foresee the risks this reality will bring. One hopes that Deutsche Bank does not suffer a fate similar to that of Austria's Credit-Anstalt in 1931 with the consequences that followed, but one cannot rule the possibility out, given that Germany is already in recession and the outlook for her weakened, undercapitalized banks is exceedingly grim.

That being the case, a new banking crisis is not only in the making, for which the repo problem serves as an early warning, but it could escalate quite rapidly. Given the rethinking that must be taking place in the boardrooms at all the major US banks, bankers will be looking at not only their exposure to Deutsche, but also the implications for their wider lending exposure to other American counterparties, particularly those owned by foreign banks.

Understanding there will be a transition of attitudes from investing in CLOs and leveraged loans to a concern over their soundness is the key to realising how a credit crisis evolves. This time, as well as a mountain of derivative contracts, there is the further problem of synthetic ETFs, many of which are sponsored and managed by the same bank. For example, Deutsche Bank controls 42 ETFs in the US market alone, worth $14.6bn, all of which appear to be synthetic.

Assuming this analysis is correct, there is probably not much the Fed can do, other than react to events. Like all central banks, the Fed relies on models that cannot incorporate the changing attitudes of market participants. Just imagine, if the Fed did spot a developing crisis in advance and called in the major bankers in an effort to get them to help stabilize the situation, they would likely leave the meeting with the clear impression things are worse than they thought, and their clear duty to their shareholders is to liquidate all positions at risk.

If it took two months between Libor freezing in December 2007 and Northern Rock being rescued by the UK government and if that timing is replicated today, a new banking crisis will hit in November. It could easily take longer to materialize, but there's no guarantee it won't escalate even more rapidly than that.

6

7 Reasons Why European Banks Are in Trouble

by Philipp Bagus

While the euro crisis seems far away as all Eurozone countries ran government deficits below 3 percent of GDP, there is one problem for the euro that quietly keeps growing: the unresolved banking crisis. And this is not a small problem. The Eurosystems' and euro banks' balance sheets totaled €30 trillion in January 2018, that is about 291 percent of GDP.

European banks are in trouble for several reasons.

First, banking regulation has become tighter after the financial crisis. As a consequence regulatory and compliance costs have risen substantially. Today banks have to fulfill demands by national authorities, the European Banking Authority, the Single Supervisory Mechanism, the European Securities and Markets Authority and the national central banks. Being at a staggering 4 percent of total revenue currently, compliance costs are expected to rise to 10 percent of total revenue until 2022.

Philipp Bagus, "7 Reasons Why European Banks Are in Trouble," *Mises Wire* (May 17, 2018).

Second, there are risks hidden in banks' balance sheets. That there is something fishy in European banks' assets can quickly be detected when comparing banks market capitalization with their book value. Most European banks have price-to-book ratios below 1. German Commerzbank's price-to-book ratio stands at 0.49, Deutsche Bank's is at 0.36, Italian UniCredit's at 0.23, Greek Piraeus Bank at 0.14, and Greek Alpha Bank at 0.34.

With a price-to-book ratio below 1, buying a bank at the current prices and liquidating its assets at book value, an investor could make profits. Why are investors not doing that? Simply, because they do not believe in the book value of the banks' assets. Assets are too optimistically valued in the eyes of market participants. Considering that the equity ratio (equity divided by balance sheet total) of the Euro banking sector is at only 8.3 percent, a down valuation of assets could quickly evaporate equity.

Third, low interest rates have contributed to increasing asset prices. Stocks and bond prices have increased due to the monetary policy of the ECB, thereby leading to accounting profits for banks. Monetary policy has, thereby, artificially propped up banking profits during the last years.

Fourth, according to the ECB non-performing loans (NPLs), i.e. loans where borrowers have fallen behind in their payments, amount to €759 bn., that is 30 percent of the banks' equity.

Fifth, more trouble for banks lies ahead. Due to artificially low interest rates, insolvency rates have fallen. In Germany in 2003, 39,470 companies (1.36 percent of existing companies) became insolvent. By 2017 insolvencies had fallen to 20,200 companies (0.62 percent).

Companies that otherwise would have had to close, can survive due to interest rates close to zero. Their survival is not without cost as they suck up resources that could be used in

Insolvency Rate in Germany 2003–2017, by percent

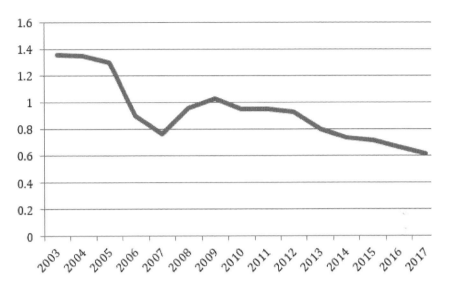

Source: Creditreform.de

other projects. Every year of the ECB's zero interest rate policy 10,000s of bankruptcies are postponed adding to a growing stock of zombie companies. The zombie companies contribute to the anemic growth because they mal use resources that could be used more productively in other lines of production. Once interest rates increase rapidly these zombie companies will come to the roost and insolvency rates will return to more normal levels leading to problems for banks.

Sixth, lower interest rates have posed severe problems to banks' net interest margin. The passive, the transformation and the credit margin of banks have fallen. The passive margin results from investing deposits of bank clients in the overnight interbank market. Banks could earn traditionally a margin this way but not in a world of negative interbank rates. The transformation margin results from maturity transformation, when a bank borrows short-term from a client and lends long-term to another client. With a flattened yield curve, this transformation yields less than it normally would. Borrowing at 0 percent in order to lend long term at 0 percent is not profitable. Moreover, when banks lend long term at very low interest rates and short-term rates start to increase, margins fall further.

The credit margin results from the risk of lending. Banks try to compensate the falling passive and transformation margin by assuming higher credit risks. The competition of banks in this field drives down the credit margin as well. Thus the zero interest rate policy of the ECB has cannibalized traditional bank profitability.

Seventh, banks in the Eurozone are still connected closely to their government. As of January 2018, Eurozone banks held €3.536 bn. Government debt on their books which amounts to 13 percent of their balance sheet total. When in the next recession, the sovereign debt crisis looms again banks can expect losses on their sovereign debt portfolio.

When interest rates increase in the future banks will be confronted with several difficulties. First, non-performing loans will increase and zombie companies will go bust. Second, banks' long term low interest rate loans will become more difficult to refinance profitably. Third, asset prices will fall leading to losses. Government may get into trouble.

As a result of these losses, banks will be forced to restrict credits as their equity shrinks. Ironically, the ECB's zero interest rate policy designed to promote credit expansion will finally lead to a credit contraction. There will be a severe recession and a fall in the money supply. The crisis will not only endanger the banking system but the euro as such, because troubled Eurozone government will try to recapitalize their banks through a monetization of newly issued debts.

7

China Is in Trouble

by Ronald-Peter Stöferle and Mark J. Valek

Before we discuss the economic situation of China, a few words about China's strongman, Xi Jinping. The "new Chinese emperor" has engineered a meteoric rise. He started off as simple rural laborer but is now the most powerful Chinese president since Deng Xiaoping. Such a career path requires strength, tact, and probably a dash of unscrupulousness.

While the rulers of China have been able all along to hedge their plans over longer periods than their Western counterparts have, the new legal situation has extended this planning horizon even further.[1] In comparison with those of Western economies, China's countermeasures against the crisis in 2008 were significantly more drastic. While in the US the balance sheet total of the banking system increased by USD 4,000bn

---

[1] An analogy from the field of sports: The national sport of the USA is baseball; in China, it is Go. The approach to foreign politics is similar: The Americans are known for their short-term "hit and run" foreign policy, whereas the Chinese play the long game in their foreign policy and are very difficult to read in doing so.

Ronald-Peter Stöferle and Mark J. Valek, "China Is in Trouble," *Mises Wire* (June 9, 2018).

in the years after the global financial crisis, the balance sheet of the Chinese banking system expanded by USD 20,000bn in the same period. For reference: This is four times the Japanese GDP.

PBoC balance sheet (USD bn)

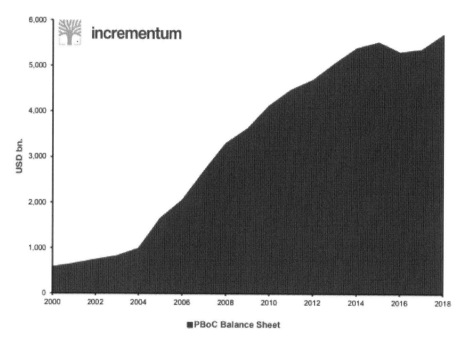

Sources: PBoC, Incrementum AG

The following chart shows the expansion of the bank balance sheet total as compared to economic output. Did the Chinese authorities assume excessive risks in fighting the crisis?

Assets of the Chinese banking system

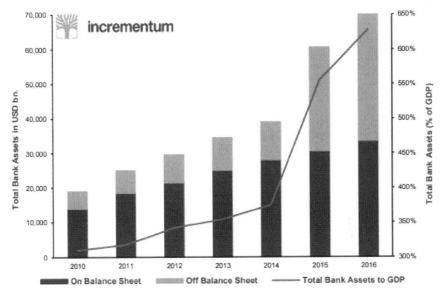

Sources: PBoC, "China Financial Stability Report 2017", Incrementum AG

Neither the fact that China's bank balance sheets amount to more than 600 percent of GDP nor the fact that they have doubled in terms of percentage of GDP in the past several years suggests a healthy development. Our friends from Condor Capital expect NPL ratios51F to rise in China, which could translate into credit losses of USD 2,700 to 3,500bn for China's banks, and this is under the assumption of no contagion (!). By comparison, the losses of the global banking system since the financial crisis have been almost moderate at USD 1,500bn

The most recent crisis does teach us, however, that the Chinese are prepared to take drastic measures if necessary. China fought the financial crisis by flooding the credit markets: 35 percent credit growth in one year on the basis of a classic Keynesian spending program is no small matter.

Credit growth in China (yoy %)

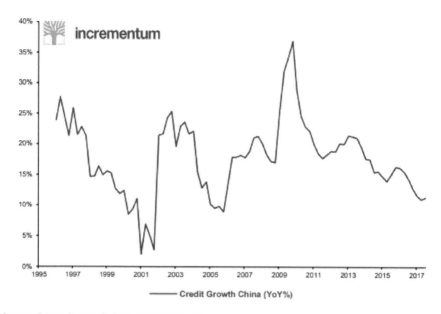

Sources: Federal Reserve St. Louis, Incrementum AG

Chinese money not only inflates a property bubble domestically but also around the globe (e.g., in Sydney and Vancouver). Further support for the global property markets is in question, given the measures China has recently launched. Due to financial problems, Chinese groups such as Anbang and HNA will have to swap the role of buyer for that of seller.

The IMF has forecast a further doubling of total Chinese debt outstanding from USD 27,000bn in 2016 to USD 54,000bn in 2022. By comparison, in 2016 China's GDP amounted to USD 11,200bn. This spells debt-induced growth at declining rates of marginal utility. From our point of view, this development—which we can also see in the West—is unsustainable.

Total debt China

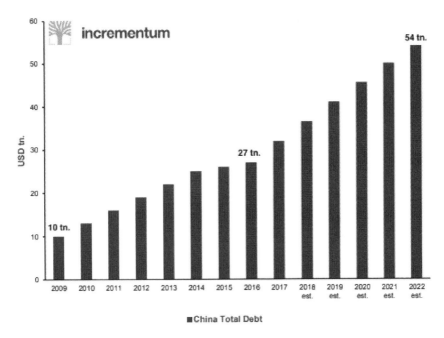

Sources: CEIC, IMF, Incrementum AG

In its most recent report, "Credit Booms—Is China different?", the IMF states that in forty-three cases worldwide of strong credit growth (i.e., the ratio of credit to GDP grows more than 30 percent over five years), only five cases ended up without a significant slowdown or a financial crisis. The IMF also points out that no expansion of credit that started at a debt to GDP ratio above 100 percent of GDP ended well. It is worth noting that China has a high percentage of domestic as opposed to foreign debt, which definitely makes matters easier for the country. But the question is: Will it be different for China this time?

The nineteenth-century Opium Wars that China fought with England, which are deeply rooted within the collective memory of the Chinese people, are historical events that are of great importance in connection with the punitive tariffs imposed by the US, as they remain a fixed and integral part of the Chinese history curriculum in schools.[2] If necessary, China could stir up anti-Western sentiment in order to implement measures that are hard on its own population, even if they are unpopular. The buck would of course stop with the Americans. Thus, the US could shoot itself in the foot with any escalation of the trade war, as we regard the ability to bear hardships and the cohesion of Chinese society as much stronger than those of the American society.

The demographic development of China is also worth a quick sidebar. The World Bank forecasts a population peak of 1.4bn for China in 2028. The decline in population that is pre-

Development of the Chinese population

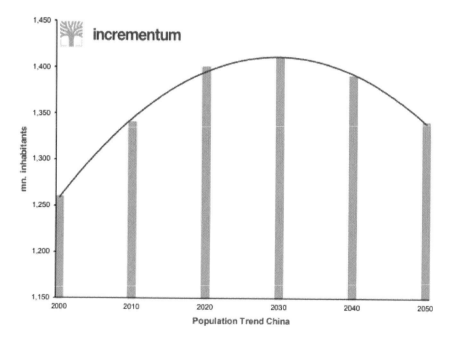

Population Trend China

Sources: World Bank, Incrementum AG

[2]Recommended reading: *The Opium Wars*, by Julia Lovell

dicted to set in around that time should proceed at a similar pace as the increase towards the peak.

The fit-for-work population (aged 16 to 59) has been decreasing since 2012 and is expected to decline by almost 25 percent to 700mn by 2050. Thus China, much like the West, has the problem of an aging population.

China's fit-for-work population

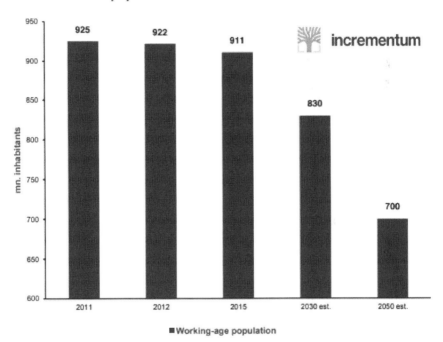

■ Working-age population

Sources: Chinese Ministry of Human Resources and Social Security, Incrementum AG

Conclusion

Unlike his Western competitors, China's new strongman, Xi, can implement his long-term strategy in a targeted and gradual fashion. Xi explicitly underlined his goal of asserting China's interests in the world by referring to military, economic, political, and diplomatic means in his speech at the National Congress in October 2017.[3] He left no doubt that China was not willing to compromise in any shape or form with regard to its territorial integrity (N.B. Taiwan, Hong Kong, Tibet), and he issued point-blank threats against separatist tendencies.

However, the transformation of the economy could (intentionally or otherwise) cause economic distortions not only in China but globally. Recent years have been dominated by a massive expansion of credit. In fact, it is often said that China has blown the biggest credit bubble in history.

It seems, there are greater similarities between China and the US than may be visible at first glance. China builds real estate for a shrinking population, invests for an overindebted client (the US, which even insists on a drastic reduction of the bilateral trade deficit) and finances all this with money it does not have.[4]

---

[3]http://www.bbc.com/news/world-asia-china-43466685

[4]A paraphrase of the famous quote from "Fight Club": "We buy things we don't need with money we don't have to impress people we don't like."

What Central Banks
May Do Next

8

How a Fragile Euro May Not Survive the Next Crisis

by Brendan Brown

A big US monetary inflation bang brought the euro into existence. Here's a prediction: It's death will occur in response to a different type of US monetary bang—the sudden emergence of a "deflationary interlude." And this could come sooner than many expect.

The explanation of this sphynx-like puzzle starts with Paul Volcker's abandonment of the road to sound money in 1985/6. The defining moment came when the then Fed Chief joined with President Reagan's new Treasury Secretary, James Baker, in a campaign to devalue the dollar. The so-called "Plaza Accord" of 1985 launched the offensive.

Volcker, the once notorious devaluation warrior of the Nixon Administration (as its Treasury under-secretary), never changed his spots, seeing large US trade deficits as dangerous. The alternative diagnosis—that in the early mid-1980s these were a transitory counterpart to increased US economic dynamism and a resurgent global demand for a now apparently hard dollar—just did not register with this top official.

Brendan Brown, "How a Fragile Euro May Not Survive the Next Crisis," *Mises Wire* (November 23, 2018).

Hence the opportunity to restore sound money. But this comes very rarely in history—only in fact, where high inflation has induced general political revulsion (as for example after the Civil War)—was inflation snuffed out. In the European context this meant the end of the brief hard-Deutsche-mark (DM) era and the birth of the soft euro.

The run-up of the DM in 1985–7 against other European currencies, as provoked by the US re-launch of monetary inflation, tipped the balance of political power inside Germany in favor of the European Monetary Union (EMU) project. The big exporting companies, the backbone of the ruling Christian Democrat Union (CDU) under Chancellor Kohl, won the day. The hard DM, an evident threat to their profits, had to go. The monetarist regime in Germany tottered towards a final collapse.

Around the globe, there was the inevitable run-up of inflation in the aftermath of the Plaza Accord and Volcker's capitulation, given that many countries (crucially Japan) sought to limit the dollar's fall against their own countries by following the US monetary lead. The inflation was evident in asset markets and good markets. Out of that new monetary chaos come an onward journey to the next stabilization experiment on both sides of the Atlantic: the "2 percent inflation standard."

Volcker in the pre-launch publicity for his new book (*Keeping At It: The Quest for Sound Money and Good Government*) now criticizes the Federal Reserve and leading foreign central banks for pursuing a 2 percent inflation target. One must wonder where he has been the last twenty years. It seems that as a monetary bureaucrat he follows the timeless rule of not in any way blaming himself for the emergence of subsequent trouble, in this case the deeply flawed 2 percent regime.

Yes, the real evil genius behind the new standard may well have been Stanley Fischer, the intellectual leader of the neo-Keynesian assault, perfectly politically timed, on monetarism. But Volcker provided the opportunity.

Birth of the ECB

At the European Central Bank (ECB), which opened its doors in late 1998, it was ex-Bundesbank official, Professor Otmar Issing, who steered Europe towards adopting the new 2 percent standard. German monetary exceptionalism came to an end; or some would say that Germany abdicated as the hard money sovereign of Europe. Under its monetary rule much of Western Europe had enjoyed considerable monetary independence from the US at least in the heydays of the mid 1970s when Arthur Burns had embarked on a second great monetary inflation.

By contrast, under the 2 percent regime, the euro zone, including Germany, aligned itself to the US monetary cycle, sharing in all the ups and downs of US inflation. And in the European context, asset inflation meant vast mal-investment most obvious in the enfeebling of Italy's once dynamic economy and a bloating of Northern Europe's export sector (reflecting an undervalued euro).

A Test for the Euro

In these two distortions we find the existential vulnerability of the euro and the next US monetary shock will present the severest test yet. The shock is most likely to take the form of a sudden arrival of a "deflationary interlude" in a long and likely intensifying monetary inflation over the long-run beyond.

Specifically, as the virulent asset inflation stoked up in the present global monetary cycle (as always led by the Federal Reserve) proceeds into the final stage of unwind (asset deflation) and recession, there will be a period of overall credit contraction. This will be reflected most likely in the broad money aggregates. Prices and wages could come under some downward pressure, though this is not in itself evidence of monetary deflation.

In this asset deflation phase, accompanied by global slow-down or recession, Europe would be in a particularly dangerous situation. The vastly over-extended export sectors of Northern Europe are vulnerable, not least to the emerging market credit bubble turning to bust. Weak banks and sovereigns across Europe would descend into an insolvency zone. The weak euro and market share boosting measures of the big northern European exporters are likely to attract Trumpian ire.

There would be zero tolerance in Washington for continued or new-style monetary radicalism in Europe. If this is what holding the euro together requires, meaning that currency's perpetual weakness, then it should not be held together.

A New, Smaller Euro Zone?

Hence the big German export companies would face a Day of Reckoning. The axis which joins the Berlin Chancellery to the ECB (at present the Merkel-Draghi axis) would no longer be able to support them (via a cheap euro). Under these changed circumstances, the euro falling apart may be their most promising road to future success. Yes, a re-incarnated DM would press down on export profit margins; but the menace of US-German or US-EU trade war would recede.

The CDU could have new scope to move towards the right and away from the prevailing euro-centrism of the Merkel era, so winning back voters from the parties on the far right while also gaining some middle-class support from savers long disgruntled with the soft euro and negative interest rate euro. The feared descent of Germany into Weimar-style political chaos as could occur if the CDU remains frozen in euro-centrism (eventually joining up with the Greens in coalition and thereby fanning support for the extreme parties) could be aborted.

Yes, Italy would fall out of the euro-zone. The potential for sound money renaissance in Europe, possibly with France,

Holland and Germany getting together in a new monetary union, would be real. Europe's monetary future would no longer hang on a US thread. This possible window of opportunity might be short, given the potential danger of a US inflation storm further ahead as stemming from devastatingly weak public finances.

.

9

Not-So-Modern Monetary Theory

by Arkadiusz Sieroń

According to some columnists, modern monetary theory (MMT) is the most powerful economic alternative to neoliberal orthodoxy. Is this really the case?

The key idea of MMT is that the government that controls the issuance of its currency cannot go bankrupt because it can always issue money to pay off its creditors. If so, then the government should not shy away from increasing the necessary expenditures. The government of a sovereign state can afford any expense—due to the currency monopoly, it cannot run out of money.

In a sense, the above description is true. The state actually has a monopoly on bank notes, so it cannot be insolvent like private individuals. That is why we hear about hyperinflation from time to time—the latest example is Venezuela, which not only exercised its monetary sovereignty, but did so on a grand scale.

Arkadiusz Sieroń, "Not-So-Modern Monetary Theory," *Mises Wire* (October 8, 2019).

The main thesis of MMT is therefore not a revolution. Neo-liberal orthodoxy, whatever it may be, acknowledges not only that the state can increase the money supply, but also its costs. This cost is, of course, inflation. And in order to minimize it, the current institutional order has been designed, in which governments cannot directly monetize their deficits (although they do this indirectly). This is not a discovery of the wheel—you can read about it in any economics textbook.

Inflation costs mean that—contrary to the popular myth professed by MMT—governments that issue and repay debt in their own currency also go bankrupt. According to the article "Sovereign defaults by currency denomination" published in the *Journal of International Money and Finance* in 2016 (vol. 60, February, pp. 197–222), defaults on local and foreign currency bonds are equally frequent—only its determinants change. The authors state that in 1996–2012, governments stopped honoring their foreign currency bonds 27 times, and their domestic currency bonds 31 times (the most-known contemporary examples are Russia in 1998, Turkey in 1999 and Argentina in 2001), which empirically falsifies MMT.

As the Fitch agency explains, governments sometimes decide not to inflate away its debt, as inflation is economically and politically costly. This cost can be so high that some countries decide on full dollarization, renouncing—oh, no!—their monetary sovereignty.

It is also worth realizing that the government's largest creditors are commercial banks. If the government stopped paying its debts, it would have a negative effect on banks and their credit action, which would ricochet throughout all the economy.

As a description of a sovereign's capacity to print money, MMT is not new. The MMT theory is, however, an erroneous description of reality, because it is too abstract from the current institutional conditions. In developed economies, commercial and central banks—not governments—create money. Although banks are certainly not fully independent from the governments, we can assume that their desire to inflate away the sovereign debts is somewhat weaker than in the case of the Treasury (the question of the relationship between the central bank and the government, especially in the context of unconventional monetary policies, is a topic for a separate article). So governments cannot in practice arbitrarily increase the money supply to finance all possible expenses, at least not without altering the current institutional constraints which exist in developed countries.

It is true that MMT recognizes the risk of inflation, but it assumes that the inflation genie can only get out of the bottle when the economy reaches full employment. But even then we should not worry, because in this case the government can easily reduce inflation by increasing taxes. Here come a few questions. First, when will it be known that the economy has achieved unobservable potential output and it is time to increase taxes? Second, why would an increase in taxes, which is transfer of money from the private to the public sector, halt inflation with the money supply unchanged? Third, what about asset price inflation and exchange rate depreciation? What about all the controversies about the Philips curve? And last but not least: why should we believe that government with unlimited monetary sovereignty will stop printing money and politely increase unpopular taxes as soon as the inflation rate exceeds an arbitrarily determined value?

Finally, I would like to point out another worrying short-coming of MMT: it seems to mistakenly identify money with capital. It is true that the state has potentially extraordinary power to print money, but money is not real capital. Banknotes or electronic records are not real wealth—they are means of exchange, as Hume or Smith have already pointed out. Only the quantity of goods and services that we can afford is important. The government can pump any amount of money into the economy—but it cannot remove the fundamental scarcity of resources and magically create new goods. Supporters of MMT complain about the scarcity of goods—but this does not stem from class interests. It is a fundamental problem of economics and its raison d'etre. The increase in money supply does not solve this problem. Inflation and the accompanying Cantillon effect ultimately only redistribute resources from one group of people to another.

The claim that MMT is the strongest alternative to the mainstream is therefore wishful thinking. An economic analysis shows that MMT is a combination of old obviousness (observation that the state has potential to increase the money supply) and new concepts (resulting implications for macroeconomics and economic policy). The problem is that, as Thomas Palley, a Post-Keynesian economist, puts it, "is a mix of old and new, the old is correct and well understood, while the new is substantially wrong." It says a lot that even prominent Post-Keynesians—people far from neoliberal orthodoxy and the desire to reduce state interventionism—do not see any value added in MMT.

10

Central Bank's Are Propping Up Stock Prices

by Thorsten Polleit

Financial markets seem to have a great deal of confidence in the effectiveness of central bank monetary policy—in the sense that by keeping interest rates low, or bring interest rates down, the economies will keep expanding and asset prices, in particular, will keep rising. There is, however, good reason for savers and investors alike to think very carefully about the truth value of such a proposition.

The key question is this: What is the actual relation between the interest rate and asset prices, stock prices in particular? To answer this question, it may be helpful to take a brief look at the well-known "Gordon Growth Model". It shows the functional relation between a firm's stock price and its profit level, the interest rate, and the firm's profit growth rate. The formula is:

stock price = $D / (i - g)$,
whereas D = dividend, i = interest rate, and g = profit growth.

Thorsten Polleit, "Central Bank's Are Propping Up Stock Prices," *Mises Wire* (April 11, 2019).

If, say, $D = 10$ US\$, $i = 5$ percent and $g = 0$ percent, the stock price is 200 US\$ [10 / (0.05 - 0) = 200]. If g then goes up to 2 percent, the stock price rises to 333.3 US\$. If the central bank lowered the interest rate to 4 percent, the stock price goes up further to 500.0 US\$. Should g then drop to 1 percent, the stock price would decline back to 333.3, and if g falls even lower to 0,005 percent, the stock price falls to 285.7.

Foreign exchange market turnover by currency and currency pairs[1]

Net-net basis, daily averages in April, in per cent   Graph 1

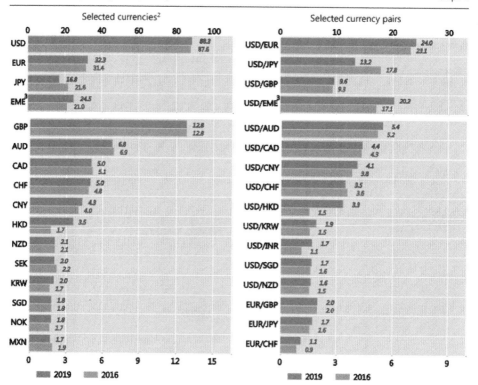

[1] Adjusted for local and cross-border inter-dealer double-counting, ie "net-net" basis.   [2] As two currencies are involved in each transaction, the sum of shares in individual currencies will total 200%.   [3] EME currencies.

Source: BIS Triennial Central Bank Survey. For additional data by currency and currency pairs, see Tables 2 and 3 on pages 10 and 11, respectively. See our Statistics Explorer for access to the full set of published data.

This little example shows that a central bank can drive up stock prices by lowering the interest rate. However, what about the effect the interest rate has on firms' profit growth? From a Keynesian viewpoint one may argue: well, lower interest rates trigger new spending, and this should increase firms' profits. While that may well be so in the short run, one might expect additional effects emerging in the longer term: namely that a policy of extremely low interest rates could sap the strength out of an economy.

For instance, artificially low interest rates keep unprofitable businesses alive, making it harder for better producers to gain market shares. This, in turn, slows down competitive pressure in factor and products markets, resulting in lower growth and employment, and ultimately deteriorating firms' profit situation. Also, low credit costs invite governments to ramp up deficit spending, diverting scarce resources into unproductive projects. The material well-being of the people remains below potential.

The above points towards an uncomfortable scenario: Central banks, via their policy of extremely low interest rates, drive up stock prices to ever higher levels. Then, at some point, investors factor in the low rate policy's counterproductive effect and revise their expectations regarding firms' future profit growth downwards. Once a stock price decline starts, it would be fairly difficult to bring it to a stop—if and when interest rates have already reached rock bottom.

Needless to say that a decline in stock prices would also most likely be a drag on other goods' prices—such as, say, raw materials, intermediate goods' and housing estate prices. A general downward shift of prices would be a heavy burden on today's unbacked paper money system—first and foremost because declining prices could trigger a massive round of credit default: As their nominal incomes decline, or fall below expectations, borrows will find it increasingly difficult to service their debt.

Return on investment for different purchase prices

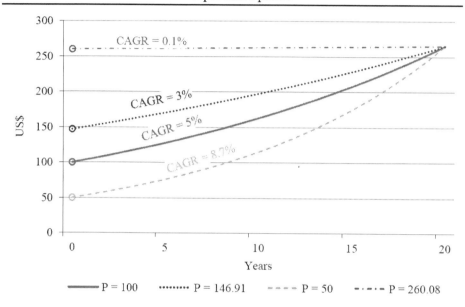

Legend: own calculations.

Note: The return on capital is 5% p.a. for the coming 20 years.

P = purchase price of the investment. CAGR = Cumulated annualized growth rate (in percent).

In the extreme case, the unbacked paper money system could even come crashing down. For if the credit market, due to default concerns, drives up borrowing costs and makes credit less accessible for borrowers, a bust is very likely. This would actually explode the economy's production and employment structure that has been set up in the period of artificially lowered interest rates.

Of course, governments and their central banks would want to prevent, by all means, such a price deflation and the ensuing crash. In this effort they can count on the support of the wider public: People simply don't like recession and unemployment. One option monetary policy-makers might have in mind is pushing interest rates (even further) into negative territory, at least in real terms. However, this might not be as easy as it seems.

For there is something called the "zero bound of nominal interest rates". It means that nominal interest rates cannot be pushed below zero. So if and when prices fall, interest rates remain positive, or even rise, in real terms. And this would certainly not stop a credit pyramid from coming crashing down. And so central banks will see just one way out: outright money printing—via asset purchases and/or issuing "helicopter money."

But who shall get the newly issued money? Should it go into the hands of consumers, or entrepreneurs, or banks, or the government? Or to all of them? And how much money should be issued? Should it be issued early or later in the month? Should everybody get the same amount or, say, a 10 percent increase of his bank deposits? What is the proper principle for distributing new quantities of money? Welcome to socialism!

The monetary policy of extremely low interest rates is far from harmless—even though it seems to support the business cycle and props up asset markets in the short-run, suggesting that all is well. There is, in fact, sound economic reason to assume that central banks' artificially low interest rate policy is self-defeating—and the risk that something will go terribly wrong increases, the longer interest rates remain at suppressed levels.

11

Will the Drive to Devalue the Dollar Lead to a Plaza Accord 2.0?

by Ronald-Peter Stöferle

The Lead-Up to the Plaza Accord

To understand the Plaza Accord, one has to look back to August 15, 1971. On this day Richard Nixon closed the gold window. This step *de facto* ended the Bretton Woods system, which had been created in 1944 in the New Hampshire town of the same name and was formally terminated in 1973. The era of gold-backed currency was well and truly over; the era of flexible exchange rates had begun. Without a gold anchor, the exchange rate of every currency pair was supposed to be driven exclusively by supply and demand. National central banks—and indirectly governments as well—were at liberty to make their own decisions, free of the tight restrictions imposed by a gold standard, but they had to bear the costs of their decisions in the form of the devaluation or appreciation of their currencies. While a gold-backed currency aims to impose discipline on nations, a system of flexible exchange rates enables national idiosyncrasies to be preserved, with the exchange rate serving as a balancing mechanism.

Ronald-Peter Stöferle, "Will the Drive to Devalue the Dollar Lead to a Plaza Accord 2.0?," *Mises Wire* (September 2, 2019).

However, unlike any other currency system, the system of free-floating currencies invites governments and central banks to manipulate exchange rates practically at will. Without reciprocal agreements, which can provide planning security to export-oriented companies in particular, the danger of international chaos is very high, as the system of flexible exchange rates lacks an external anchor.

In order to prevent this chaos, a repetition of the traumatic devaluation spiral of the 1930s, and the resulting disintegration of the global economy, IMF member nations agreed in 1976 at a meeting in Kingston, Jamaica, that *"the exchange rate should be economically justified. Countries should avoid manipulating exchange rates in order to avoid the need to regulate the balance of payments or gain an unfair competitive advantage."*[1] And in this multilateral spirit—albeit under a US initiative that was strongly tinged by self-interest—an agreement was struck nine years later that has entered the economic history books as the Plaza Accord.

Macroeconomic Excesses in the 1980s?

In the first half of the 1980s the US dollar appreciated significantly against the most important currencies. In five years the dollar rose by around 150 percent against the French franc, almost 100 percent against the Deutschmark, and intermittently 34.2 percent against the yen (from the January 1981 low).

The significant appreciation of the US dollar was of course reflected in the US Dollar Index, which consists of the currencies of the most important US trading partners, weighted according to their share of trade with the US. The following

[1]"The Specificity of the Jamaica Monetary System," ebrary.net; see also article IV (iii) of the "Articles of Agreement of the International Monetary Fund."

chart, moreover, shows exchange rates in real terms—i.e., it takes price levels into account, which can vary substantially in some cases.

Real trade-weighted US Dollar Index,
03/1973=100, 01/1980–12/1989

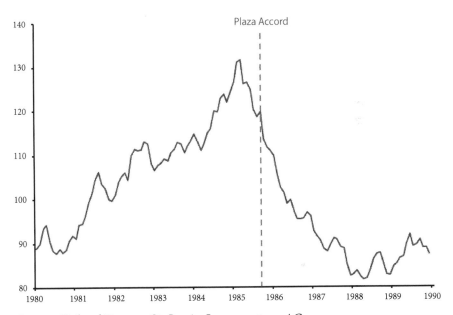

Source: Federal Reserve St. Louis, Incrementum AG

From an interim low of 87.7 in July 1980, the index rose by about 50 percent to 131.6 by March 1985. Not surprisingly, the US current account balance deteriorated significantly in the first half of the 1980s as a result of this substantial dollar rally, as the following chart shows.

Current account balance, US, Germany, France, United Kingdom, Japan, in % of GDP, 1980–1989

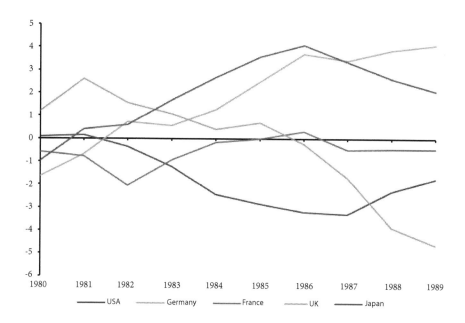

Source: World Bank, Quandl, Incrementum AG

In 1980 and 1981 the US still posted a moderate surplus, but by 1985 this surplus had turned into a deficit of 2.9 percent. The trend in Germany and Japan was almost a perfect mirror image. While the two export nations had current account deficits of 1.7 percent and 1.0 percent in 1980, their current account balances turned positive in 1981 and 1982, respectively. In 1985, they already posted surpluses of 2.5 percent and 3.6 percent. Germany's current account surplus in particular grew even further in subsequent years.

The Plaza Accord

Representatives of the US, Germany, Japan, France, and Great Britain, a.k.a. the G5 countries, met in September 1985 at the

Plaza Hotel in New York under the leadership of US Treasury Secretary James Baker in order to coordinate their economic policies. Their declared aim was to reduce the US current account deficit, which they planned to accomplish by weakening the overvalued US dollar. Moreover, the US urged Germany and Japan to strengthen domestic demand by expanding their budget deficits, which was supposed to give US exports a shot in the arm.

In the Plaza Accord, the five signatory nations agreed to cooperate more closely when cooperation made sense. The criterion cited for adopting a joint approach was "deviation from fundamental economic conditions." Interventions in the foreign exchange market were to be conducted with the aim of combating current account imbalances. In the short term the target was a 10–12 percent devaluation of the US dollar relative to its level of September 1985.

The immediate outcome of the agreement was as desired. One week after the Plaza Accord had been signed, the Japanese yen gained 11.8 percent against the US dollar, while the German mark and the French franc gained 7.8 percent each, and the British pound 2.8 percent. However, the speed of the adjustment in foreign exchange markets continued to be the same as before the Plaza agreement, as the following chart clearly shows.

USD exchange rate vs. DEM, FRF, JPY, GBP, 01/01/1980=100, 01/1980–09/1985

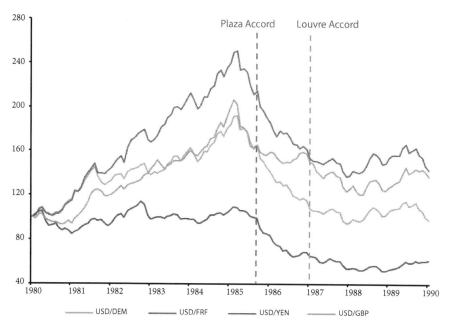

Source: fxtop.com, Incrementum AG

However, the charts also show quite clearly that the depreciation of the US dollar had already begun several months *before* the official agreement was concluded in the heart of Manhattan. The Dollar Index had reached its peak in March of 1985, i.e., half a year before the Plaza Accord.

Plaza Accord 2.0?

Some people propose the creation of a new version of the Plaza Accord, i.e., a multilateral agreement that includes, *inter alia*, coordinated intervention in foreign exchange markets. The proponents of a Plaza Accord 2.0 point to the appreciation of the US dollar by almost 40 percent (particularly in the years 2011–2016), and to the large differences between the current account balances of the leading developed countries. However, such an agreement would represent a new turning point in international currency policy. After all, in 2013 the G8 agreed to refrain from foreign exchange interventions—in a kind of Anti-Plaza Accord.[2]

The following chart illustrates the significant appreciation of the US dollar in recent years.

**Real trade-weighted US Dollar Index,
03/1973 = 100, 01/2011–04/2019**

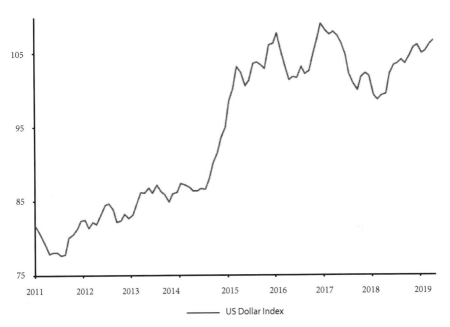

Source: Federal Reserve St. Louis, Incrementum AG

[2]"The Plaza Accord, 30 Years Later" by Jeffrey Frankel, *NBER Working Paper* No. 21813, Issued in December 2015.

And just as was the case thirty years ago, the US has a significant and persistent current account deficit, while Germany, Japan—and these days also China—have significant surpluses. Germany's surplus, which intermittently reached almost 9 percent, is particularly striking.

Current account balances of US, Germany, France, Great Britain, Japan, China, in Percent of GDP, 2010–2017

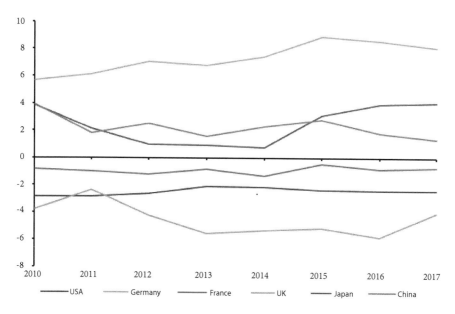

Source: World Bank, Quandl, Incrementum AG

Long before Donald Trump weighed in on the issue, the US Treasury—which is in charge of the US dollar's external value —repeatedly stressed that the dollar was too strong, especially compared to the renminbi. Time and again the US accused China, Japan, and the eurozone of keeping their currencies at artificially low levels in order to support their export industries.[3] The fact that Donald Trump used the term *manipulation* in a tweet came as a bit of a surprise, as the US has not used this term officially since 1994.[4]

In any case, such a significant adjustment in exchange rates would have to be implemented gradually; the risk of creating further distortions would be too great. An abrupt adjustment of rates might result in, for example, a significant increase in the pace of US inflation and/or a collapse of the export sectors of countries whose currencies would appreciate.

But as exchange rates—at least in the medium to long term —are mainly determined by fundamentals, exchange rates can change substantially only if underlying macroeconomic conditions (real interest rate differentials, trade and current account balances, the investment climate, and budget balances) change. Regardless of how powerful a government or how watertight an international agreement is, those who enter an agreement cannot get past this fact. As Eugen von Böhm-Bawerk has stated explicitly: "The most imposing dictate of power can never effect anything in contradiction to the economic laws of value, price, and distribution; it must always be in conformity with these; it cannot invalidate them; it can merely confirm and fulfill them."

[3]See "U.S. tensions rise over China's currency policy," CNN, October 7, 2011; "U.S. declines to name China currency manipulator," *Reuters*, November 27, 2012.

[4]Donald Trump: Tweet, July 20, 2018.

12

Negative Interest Rates are the Price We Pay for De-Civilization

by Jeff Deist

Do central bankers really think negative interest rates are rational?

"Calculation Error," which Bloomberg terminals sometimes display, is an apt metaphor for the current state of central bank policy. Both Europe and Asia are now awash in $13 trillion worth of negative-yielding sovereign and corporate bonds, and Alan Greenspan suggests negative interest rates soon will arrive in the US. Despite claims by both Mr. Trump and Fed Chair Jerome Powell concerning the health of the American economy, the Fed's Open Market Committee moved closer to negative territory today—with another quarter-point cut in the Fed Funds rate, below even a measly 2 percent.

Negative interest rates are just the latest front in the post-2008 era of "extraordinary" monetary policy. They represent a Hail Mary pass from central bankers to stimulate more borrowing and more debt, though there is far more global debt

Jeff Deist, "Negative Interest Rates are the Price We Pay for De-Civilization," *Mises Wire* (September 18, 2019).

today than in 2007. Stimulus is the assumed goal of all economic policy, both fiscal and monetary. Demand-side stimulus is the mania bequeathed to us by Keynes, or more accurately by his followers. It is the absurd idea, that an economy prospers by consuming and borrowing instead of producing and saving. Negative interest rates turn everything we know about economics upside down.

Under what scenario would anyone lend $1,000 to receive $900 in return at some point in the future? Only when the alternative is to receive $800 back instead, due to the predicted interventions of central banks and governments. Only then would locking in a set rate of capital loss make sense. By "capital loss" I mean just that; when there is no positive interest paid, the principal itself must be consumed. There is no "market" for negative rates. The future is uncertain, and there is always counterparty risk. The borrower might abscond, or default, or declare bankruptcy. Market conditions might change during the course of the loan, driving interest rates higher to the lender's detriment. Inflation could rise higher and faster than the agreed-upon nominal interest rate. The lender might even die prior to repayment.

Positive interest rates compensate lenders for all of this risk and uncertainty. Interest, like all economics, ultimately can be explained by human nature and human action.

If in fact negative interest rates can occur naturally, without central bank or state interventions, then economics textbooks need to be revised on the quick. Every theory of interest contemplates positive interest paid on borrowed capital. Classical economists and their "Real" theory say interest represents a "return" on capital, not a penalty. Capital available for lending, like any other good, is subject to real forces of supply and demand. But nobody would "sell" their capital by giving the buyer interest payments as well, they would simply hold onto it and avoid the risk of lending.

Marxists think interest payments represent exploitation by capital owners lending to needful workers. The amount of interest paid in addition to the capital returned was stolen from the debtor, because the lender did not work for it (ignoring, of course, the capitalist lender's risk). But how could a borrower be exploited by receiving interest *payments* for borrowing, i.e., repaying less than they borrowed? I suppose Marxists may in fact cheer the development of negative rates, and perversely see them as a transfer of wealth from lenders to borrowers (when, in fact, we know cheap money and credit overwhelmingly benefit wealthy elites, per the Cantillon Effect). So negative rates require Marxists to drastically rethink their theory of interest.

Austrians stress the time element of interest rates, comparing the lender's willingness to forego present consumption against the borrower's desire to pay a premium for present consumption. In Austrian theory interest rates represent the price at which the relative time preferences of lenders and borrowers meet. But once again, negative interest rates cannot explain how or why anyone would ever defer consumption without payment—or in fact pay to do so!

It should be noted that rational purchasers of negative-yield bonds hope to sell them before maturity, i.e., they hope bond *prices* rise as interest rates drop even lower. They hope to sell their bonds to a greater fool and generate a capital gain. They are not "buying" the obligation to pay interest, but the chance of reselling for a profit. So purchasing a negative-yield bond might make sense as an investment (vs. institutional and central bank bond buyers, which frequently hold bonds to maturity and thereby literally pay to lend money). But if and when interest rates rise, the losses to those left holding those $13 trillion of bonds could be staggering.

In the meantime, a huge artificial market for at least nominally positive US Treasury debt grows, strengthening the dollar and suppressing interest rates here at home. Once again, the dollar represents the least dirty shirt in the laundry. Congress loves this, of course, because even 5 percent rates would blow the federal budget to smithereens. Rising rates would cause debt service to be the largest annual line item in that budget, ahead of Social Security, Medicare, and defense. So we might say Congress and the Fed are in a symbiotic relationship at this point. The rest of the world might call it America's "exorbitant privilege."

Negative interest rates are the price we pay for central banks. The destruction of capital, economic and otherwise, is contrary to every human impulse. Civilization requires accumulation and production; de-civilization happens when too many people in a society borrow, spend, and consume more than they produce. No society in human history previously entertained the idea of negative interest rates, so like central bankers we are all in uncharted territory now.

Our job, among many, is to bring the insights of Austrian economics on money and banking to widespread attention before something truly calamitous happens.

13

What Will It Take to Get the Public to Embrace Sound Money?

by Brendan Brown

In the last decade, the combination of virulent asset price inflation and low reported consumer price inflation crippled sound money as a political force in the US and globally. In the new decade, a different balance between monetary inflation's "terrible twins"—asset inflation and goods inflation—will create an opportunity for that force to regain strength. Crucial, however, will be how sound money advocacy evolves in the world of ideas and its success in forming an alliance with other causes that could win elections.

It is very likely that the deflationary nonmonetary influences of globalization and digitalization, which camouflaged the activity of the goods-inflation twin during the past decade, are already dissipating.

The pace of globalization may have already peaked, before the Xi-Trump tariff war. Inflation-fueled monetary malinvestment surely contributed to its prior speed. One channel here

Brendan Brown, "What Will It Take to Get the Public to Embrace Sound Money?" *Mises Wire* (January 16, 2020).

was the spread of highly speculative narratives about the wonders of global supply chains.

Digitalization's potential to camouflage monetary inflation in goods and services markets, on the other hand, has come largely via its impact on the dynamics of wage determination. It has forged star firms with considerable monopoly power in each industrial sector. Obstacles preventing their technological and organizational know-how from seeping out to competitors means that wages are not bid higher across labor markets in similar fashion to earlier industrial revolutions. These obstacles reflect the fact that much investment is now in the form of firm-specific intangibles. Even so, such obstacles tend to lose their effectiveness over time.

As deflation fades, monetary repression taxes (collected for governments through central banks' manipulation of rates to low levels so as to achieve 2 percent inflation despite disinflation as described) will undergo metamorphosis into open inflation taxes as the rate of consumer price inflation accelerates. Governments cannot forego revenue given their ailing finances. Simultaneously, asset inflation will proceed down a new stretch of highway where many crashes occur.

Historical Circumstances that Help Sound Money Advocates

If the small sample size of monetary history is any guide, the combination of asset market crashes and high goods inflation empowers sound money forces in the political arena. Widespread public resentment against higher goods and services prices and wealth loss (whether by strong inflation or crash) is responsible for the shift.

By contrast, when the goods-inflation twin is camouflaged (as during the 2010s) and asset inflation is rife, unhappiness among some savers about the monetary repression tax is more than matched (in terms of electoral impact) by happiness among large segments of the population about rising wealth and the comforting performance of their pension funds.

If the asset inflation ends without the goods-inflation twin emerging from its camouflage, then most likely there would be a further triumph for unsound money, as was the case in the 1930s and again in the aftermath of the 2008 crash. The bankers, mortgage brokers, and securities salespersons would be blamed, not the money printers, though the latter's political masters might suffer the consequences even without direct attribution.

The last time we had the combination of high goods inflation coupled with crash-prone asset markets was in the later stages of the great monetary inflation from the early 1960s to the 1970s. Sound money did become a political force both in Europe and the US despite the most effective groupings' advancement of the flawed doctrines of monetarism.

The seriousness of the flaws and whether these could be lessened by various forms of financial system reconstruction were never put to the test. In the US, the Reagan administration by 1985 had decided on a new devaluation policy (highlighted by the Plaza Accord), endorsed at the start by then Fed chairman Paul Volcker. Earlier the same administration had undermined the original purpose of a commission to study a return to the gold standard (law signed by President Carter in 1980) by packing it with opponents. In Europe, the dollar devaluation of the mid-1980s created the political dynamics towards monetary union which proved fatal to discount margin (DM) monetarism.

After the waxing and waning of monetarism, the US adopted gradually the 2 percent inflation standard built on emperor's-new-clothes econometrics and expectations inertia. The newly established European Monetary Union followed suit. This all occurred just as nonmonetary deflationary forces were gaining power. At first globalization was the strongest force; later it was digitalization and resource abundance (especially of shale oil and gas).

A Sound Money Resurgence?

As the camouflage of goods and services inflation now thins, a climb in consumer price inflation may undermine the equity market and lead to an early dose of asset deflation. Governments will then double down on money printing. If that asset deflation nonetheless leads to great depression, sound money advocacy will remain dead.

However, if there is no great depression and goods inflation picks up sharply into the next cycle beyond a normal recession, sound money will have its chance. The extent of malinvestment during the monetary inflation of the past decades will be revealed in the wake of asset price deflation. Effective capital shortage resulting from the obsolescence of malinvestment will mean that goods and services price inflation can pick up faster and earlier than much conventional macroeconomic modeling would suggest as the business cycle upswing gets under way.

In this case there will still be a problem for sound money advocacy in the political arena. We can count the number of US senators in favor of sound money on one hand—and less in European parliaments. There is no ready popular brand of ideology of sound money analogous to Friedman's 1970s monetarism.

Popular branding is difficult. The fundamental prerequisite to monetary soundness is an anchoring of the monetary system, which is accomplished by designing a monetary base for which a broad and stable demand exists that is not hugely sensitive to small changes in interest rates. This is not an easy concept to popularize. Successful anchoring means that automatic mechanisms would keep money under control without any official setting or manipulation of interest rates or any targeting of the price level.

It is hard to imagine a brand "catching on" that does not include gold. which has potential and actual popular appeal. A natural ally of sound money forces promoting this brand could be antimonopolists, found on both sides of the aisle. Big Tech and Big Finance are joining with Big Government in pursuing the war against cash. While this rages, gold money and the little saver stand little chance.

In Europe the forces of sound money would have a natural base in Germany, Holland, Belgium, and Austria. These forces could build on resentment toward transfers to southern Europe and negative rates. The main counterforce for now are the Greens. Watch how European Central Bank chief Lagarde is playing to the Green Party in Germany, expecting it to be an equal partner to the Christian Democrats in the next government, probably at some point in 2020.

A gold-backed euro based in northern Europe seems like fantasy for now, but it is more plausible than a gold dollar as an outcome of this decade.

14

Yes, the Fed Really Is Holding Down Interest Rates

by Joseph T. Salerno

The very sluggish recovery of the economy since the financial crisis—despite zero and near zero interest rates—presents the dominant school of New Keynesian macroeconomists with a conundrum. Many have attempted to resolve the riddle by arguing that such unprecedentedly low interest rates are not the doing of the Fed and therefore do not indicate an expansionary monetary policy. Although not formally a New Keynesian, George Selgin has taken up and vigorously defended this position. According to Selgin, the view that interest rates have been "held down" by "the Fed's easy money policies" is based on a "myth." "The unvarnished truth," according to Selgin, "is that interest rates have been low since the last months of 2008, not because the Fed has deliberately kept them so, but in large part owing to its misguided attempt, back in 2008, to keep them from falling in the first place." Indeed, in Selgin's view, the Fed's monetary policy actually has been "too tight" since 2008.

Joseph T. Salerno, "Yes, the Fed Really Is Holding Down Interest Rates," *Mises Wire* (June 26, 2017).

Let us analyze Selgin's argument, which consists of a number of empirical and theoretical claims. We'll start with his empirical claims. Selgin contends that the policy of "quantitative easing" (QE) "represented an easing of monetary policy only in a *ceteris paribus* sense." That is, QE would have expanded the money supply had it not been neutralized by other Fed policies. These policies include the payment of interest on excess reserves (IOER) and the Treasury's Supplementary Financing Program (SPF), which either increased the demand by commercial banks for the reserves that the Fed was creating (IOER), or funneled them into a special Treasury account held at the Fed (SPF). Now it is certainly true that in theory these programs could offset or even reverse the expansionary effect of QE on the money supply. But it is easy to determine the actual effect of these programs by simply examining the data on the growth rates of monetary aggregates since 2008. Curiously, rather than following this obvious and simple procedure, Selgin presents a single chart showing the changes in total deposits at Federal Reserve banks held by the Treasury under the Supplementary Financing Account, commenting, "At one point...the SPF program alone immobilized almost $559 billion in base money preventing it from serving as a basis for private-sector [i.e., fractional-reserve bank] money creation." But Selgin's chart shows that this large neutralization of reserves only occurred for a few months in 2008, and never sidelined more than $200 billion in reserves from 2009 until the early 2011 when the program was terminated. More important, this chart gives us no indication whatsoever of the net effect of the combination of QE and the countervailing programs on monetary growth.

In fact, as we can see from Chart 1, for the nearly six years from mid-2011 to 2017, the year-over-year (YOY) growth rates of M2 and MZM varied between 5 percent and 10 percent. Selgin does concede that the IOER policy failed to prevent the effective fed funds rate from declining to the "zero bound," although he counters that it did succeed in encouraging banks to hoard some of the newly created reserves instead of using them to purchase assets and thereby create new money. But once again the question must be asked: why doesn't Selgin just directly examine the variations in the growth rates of the money supply since 2008? It is noteworthy that the rates of monetary growth during the later period are comparable to and may slightly exceed the rates during the run-up of the housing bubble from the beginning of 2002 through 2005.

CHART 1

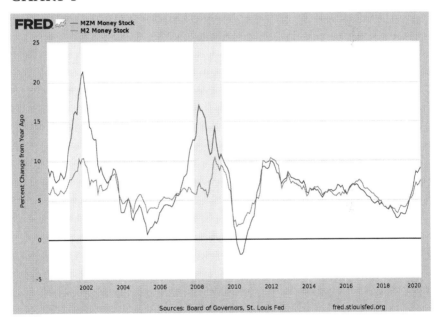

Another one of Selgin's empirical claims that can easily be tested against the data is that there is no evidence that the Fed has been following an "easy monetary policy," because monetary ease must lead to "an eventual increase in nominal spending, if not the rate of inflation. Yet, as everyone knows, neither of these things happened." Selgin then goes on to display charts showing that GDP growth was negative between September 2008 and the same month in 2009 and that the inflation rate fell to either 1.00 percent or into negative territory (if we exclude food and energy) for six months beginning with March 2009. Yet his charts take us only to the end of 2009, which hardly tests Selgin's claim that the Fed did not pursue a policy of monetary ease because an "an *eventual increase*" in GDP, i.e., nominal spending, and inflation never occurred. (Emphasis added.)

As Chart 2 shows, almost immediately after the period that Selgin considers, the YOY growth rate of GDP spurted up to nearly 5 percent. Between 2010 and 2017 it fluctuated in a range between 2.5 percent and 5.0 percnet. By Selgin's standards, this is surely evidence of an expansionary monetary policy. Indeed, in his book, *Less Than Zero*, Selgin (1997, pp. 64–66) calls for stabilizing the growth rate of nominal GDP at 0 percent per annum, thus allowing the price level to naturally decline in response to increases in labor (or total-factor) productivity induced by technological progress and capital accumulation.

CHART 2

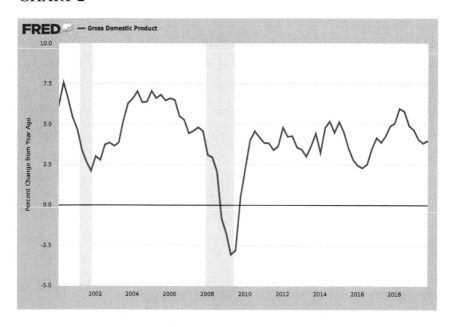

And, indeed, as we see in Chart 3, outside of the period encompassing the end of the Great Recession and its immediate aftermath, the only period for which the CPI was at or slightly below zero occurred in the first nine months of 2015, when oil prices tanked. For most of the rest of the period the inflation rate fluctuated between one 1 percent and 2 percent, with two multi-month spikes into the 2–3 percent range and one spike into 3-4 percent range.

CHART 3

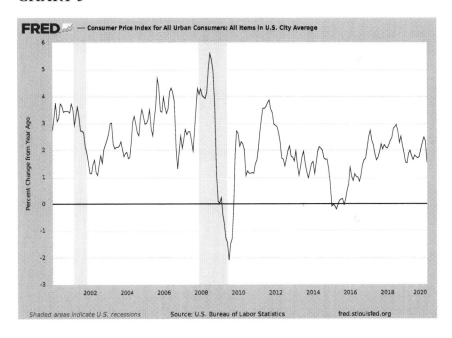

We should also note that positive inflation rates occurred in the face of a sustained fall in velocity of the monetary aggregates M2 and MZM which began in 2006, as shown in chart 4. Had the Fed merely offset this "demand-side shock," to use New Keynesian terminology, as Selgin urges in *Less Than Zero*, then the inflation rate should have been negative to reflect growth of labor productivity at an average annual rate of 1.2 percent (chart 5). Thus the US economy since 2009 has cer-

CHART 4

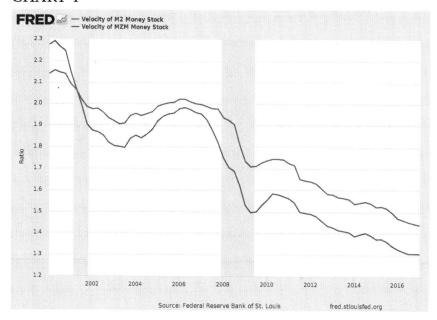

CHART 5

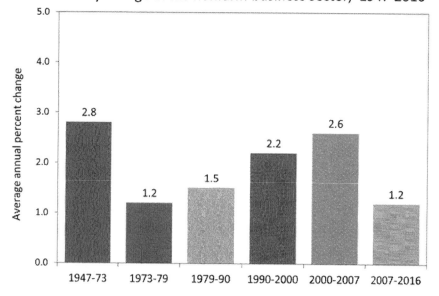

tainly experienced "relative inflation," which Selgin (1997, p. 55) defines as "output prices rising relative to unit costs." But Selgin gives no explanation of how such a relative—and for most of the period, absolute—inflation could develop and be sustained for seven years absent expansionary monetary policy by the Fed.

Given these data, we must therefore reject Selgin's empirically-based conclusion that the Fed was not engaged in expansionary monetary policy after the financial crisis and that its

> ...unprecedented asset purchases, which might ordinarily have been expected to result in roughly proportional increases in broad money, spending, inflation, and nominal interest rates, affected those variables only modestly, if at all, and did so for the most part by limiting their tendency to decline, rather than by raising them in an absolute sense.

Broad money, nominal spending, and prices did undergo a sustained and progressive rise in absolute terms during a period when velocity was steadily declining and labor productivity was increasing, which according to Selgin himself indicates a monetary easing.

In addition to the empirical flaws in his case, Selgin dismisses the application of the "(relatively) tried and true" analysis of the central bank's policy of driving down the interest rate below its natural level. This is Wicksell's analysis of the cumulative process and Selgin seems to be confused about the empirical implications and the conceptual foundations of the theory. Regarding the empirical implications, Selgin quotes Larry White:

> If the central bank wants to *keep* the market rate low in the face of the nominal income effect, it must *accelerate* the monetary injection. Short-term real rates have been negative, and nominal rates near zero, for eight

years now, with little signs of accelerating broad money growth or a rising inflation rate. .

Based on this reasoning, White, with Selgin presumably in accord, dismisses "the Wicksellian cumulative-process scenario...as a viable candidate for explaining why current rates have remained so low since 2008."

Now, White's description of the cumulative process does not accord with Wicksell's. For Wicksell, the continuation of the process does *not* require "accelerating monetary growth," which implies "a rising inflation rate." The claim that Wicksell (2007, pp. 196, 201) makes is much more modest:

> [T]he rise in prices, whether small or great at first, can never cease so long as the cause which gave rise to it continues to operate; in other words so long as the loan rate remains below the normal rate....A lowering of the loan rate below the natural rate...in itself tends to bring about a progressive rise in all commodity prices.

Elsewhere Wicksell (p. 148) comments on his model of the cumulative process: "It is possible in this way to picture a steady, and more or less uniform, rise in all wages rents, and prices (as expressed in money)."

Thus, in Wicksell's analysis, the divergence between the two rates implies only a cumulative rise in the price *level* and thus in the *level* of the money supply at a "steady" rate, and not necessarily a continual rise in the *rate* of inflation and the rate of monetary growth. In his presentation of Wicksell's model, Carl Uhr (pp. 235–41) demonstrates that the cumulative process can continue indefinitely with a constant 1.00 percent per year increase in nominal income and in the price level. Thus, White's "nominal income effect" requires only a level change in the quantity of money and prices, and not a rate change in these variables. This is clear in the "one reservation" that Wicksell expressed about his model, according to Uhr (p.

241): "namely, that the entire sequence was predicated on the assumption that entrepreneurs and others act and react only to prices current in their planning periods." It is only when inflationary expectations are introduced, according to Wicksell, that "the actual rise will become more and more rapid." We may conclude, then, that the dynamics of Wicksellian cumulative process are completely consistent with the data presented in the charts above.

This brings us to Selgin's view that the natural rate is fundamentally unobservable and must be inferred from "a mass of empirical studies." Thus Selgin cites a graph referred to by Janet Yellen which indicates that the natural rate has been negative since 2008. But this is a case of mistaken identity. For the rate that Selgin identifies is not Wicksell's natural rate but Keynes's concept of the "neutral" or "optimum" rate. In fact, Keynes explicitly rejected the Wicksellian natural rate as not "very useful or significant." Unfortunately, today, the terms "neutral rate" and "natural rate" are used interchangeably to designate the rate that was considered of policy significance by Keynes. When Bernanke, Krugman, Yellen, and other New Keynesians refer to the natural rate, they have in mind the interest rate that is consistent with full employment of resources at some targeted, non-accelerating inflation rate. The goal of the central bank is to discover and establish this fictional rate in financial markets, which will in turn drive investment spending and the real rate of return on investment to levels consistent with stability of the real economy.

This New Keynesian notion of the natural rate contrasts sharply with Wicksell's conception. According to Wicksell (p. 205), who was a follower of Böhm-Bawerk and an Austrian capital theorist, "the natural rate of interest [is] the real yield of capital in production." The natural rate is thus an "intertemporal" price, or the ratio of prices between present consumption and future consumption (as embodied in capital goods), and it is wholly and directly determined by capital investment in the real sector of the economy. The loan rate of interest is therefore a reflection of the natural rate. As Wicksell (p. 192) put it: "That loan rate that is a direct expression of the real rate, we call the normal rate." This "normal" or "natural" loan rate derives from the natural rate of return on investment throughout the economy's capital structure and moves in near lock-step with it: "The rate of interest at which *the demand for loan capital and the supply of savings exactly agree...*more or less corresponds to the expected yield on the newly created capital." (Most of this paragraph is drawn from an earlier publication of mine.)

There is thus no need to undertake econometric and other empirical studies to determine the natural rate. The natural interest rate is nothing but the basic or long-run rate of return on investment in the real structure of production. This fundamental or, what Mises called, "originary" interest rate governs the rate of interest on financial markets, not the other way around, as Keynes and his modern disciples would have it. For Wicksell and the Austrians, it is the real economy dog that wags the financial sector tail. Consequently, any and all attempts by central banks to lower the interest rate via monetary policy inevitably create a divergence between the actual and natural interest rates and initiate Wicksell's inflationary cumulative process. A complete cessation of Fed open market operations would soon enough allow the underlying interest rate on all financial instruments to return to its natural level in line with the basic rate of return on real investment as dictated by people's voluntary consumption/saving preferences.

But what of Selgin's and the New Keynesians' assertion that the notional natural rate itself has plunged through the zero bound and, therefore, the inflationary Wicksellian cumulative process does not apply, because the Fed does not yet have the tools to push the nominal rate far enough below zero. First, this assertion is absurd on its face, because it is tantamount to the claim that capitalists are investing in real capital goods at a negative rate of return, despite the existence of the universal law of time preference.

Second, we do not need "a mass of empirical studies" to confirm that the natural rate has not plunged into negative territory and may have even risen above its pre-crisis level. Consider the chart below, which appears in a publication by the U.S. Bureau of Economic Analysis (BEA) and is constructed from data in the US national income and product accounts (NIPAs). The top panel plots annual average before tax and after tax rates of return for US nonfinancial corporations for the period 1960–2015. These rates are calculated as the ratio of the net surplus of the corporation to its net stock of produced assets (i.e., capital assets plus inventories valued at current cost). The numerator of the ratio is net operating surplus which is the sum of corporate profits and a few minor items. Corporate profits are a composite of what the economist would call pure or entrepreneurial profit and the return to capital investment (the postponement of consumption). Most of "corporate profits" consist of the normal or natural return to capital investment since pure profits net to zero in a "stationary" or no-growth economy and are slightly positive in the slowly progressing US economy, where saving, investment, and real output per capita is growing slowly. Note that the after tax average rate of return hit a decadal high of 7.6 percent in 2006 and then fell for the rest of the decade to a low of 6.2 percent in 2009. It then rose sharply in 2010 to 7.9 percent and has remained at 8.0 percent or above through 2015. These variations certainly do not bespeak a collapse of the natural rate after the financial crisis.

The same story is told by a data series calculated by the BEA from industry economic accounts (IEAs), which consists of average annual rates of return for the seventy-one industries that account for all U.S. economic activity. These return

CHART 6

Rates of Return and Shares of Net Value Added for Nonfinancial Corporations, 1960–2015

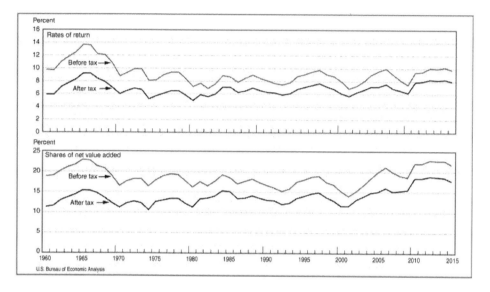

ratios are calculated as net operating surplus divided by the net stock of produced assets for each industry sector. Since the rates of return are calculated for entire industries, the numerator includes both corporate profits and the income of sole proprietorships and partnerships, so there is a significant wage component that inflates rates of return. But it is the variations in the rates of return that are significant. For this series, which is not charted, the decadal rate of return peaks in 2005 at 14.1 percent and then plunges to 11.7 percent by 2009, after which it rises rapidly to 13.3 percent in 2010 and fluctuates between 13.0 and 13.6 percent through 2015.

To summarize: George Selgin makes three strong, empirically testable claims. First, under current conditions the Fed is incapable of controlling interest rates. Second, the Fed itself is responsible for its own impotence because its monetary policy has been "too tight" since 2008. Third, zero and near-zero interest rates are not indicative of expansionary monetary policy but of a Fed-induced collapse of the natural interest rate to less than zero by tight-money policy. Based on the data adduced above in conjunction with a proper understanding of Wicksell's analysis of the natural rate, we are compelled to reject these claims as false. As noted above, a definitive empirical test of Selgin's central contention—that the super-low interest rates we are experiencing are not caused by expansionary monetary policy—would involve the termination of all open market operations. Somehow, I doubt Selgin would approve of such a test.

15

Why Government Hates Cash

by Joseph T. Salerno

In April it was announced that Greece was imposing a surcharge for all cash withdrawals from bank accounts to deter citizens from clearing out their accounts. So now the Greeks will have to pay one euro per 1,000 euros that they withdraw, which is one-tenth of a percent. It doesn't seem very big, but the *principle* at work is extremely big because what they're in effect doing is breaking the exchange rate between a unit of bank deposits and a unit of currency.

Why would they do this? Why would they *want* to do this? Well, it's one of the anti-cash policies that mainstream economists have vigorously been promoting.

Paving the Way for Negative Interest

To make the calculations easier, and to illustrate the effect, let's say that the Greek "surcharge" is ten dollars for every 100 dollars withdrawn. Now, instead of being able to convert one euro

Joseph T. Salerno, "Why Government Hates Cash," *The Austrian* 1, no. 4 (July/August 2015). This article was adapted from a talk delivered at the New York Area Mises Circle in Stamford, Connecticut.

in your checking account into one euro in cash, on demand, you will only be able to buy one euro in cash by spending 1.10 euros in your bank accounts. That's a negative 10 percent rate in some sense. That is to say that you can only take out one euro from the bank if you're willing to pay 1.10 euros. So, you would only really get ninety cents for every dollar that you wanted to withdraw and that's very significant because this means it will be more expensive to buy an item with cash than with bank deposits.

At the same time, the Greek government made it very clear that if you deposit the cash in the banks, you don't get 1.10 euros of bank money for every euro you deposit.

So the system is now structured to lock the money in the banks. Now, what does that allow them to do? If you lose 10 percent every time you withdraw one euro in cash, they can lower the interest rate that you get on bank deposits to negative 5 percent, or negative 6 percent. You still wouldn't withdraw your cash from the banks even if the interest rate went negative.

What we are witnessing is a war on cash in which governments make it either illegal or inconvenient to use cash. This, in turn, allows governments the ability to spy on and regulate financial transactions more completely, while also allowing governments more leeway in manipulating the money supply.

The Origins of the War on Cash

It all started really with the Bank Secrecy Act of 1970, passed in the US, which requires financial institutions in the United States to assist US government agencies in detecting and preventing money laundering. That was the rationale. Specifically, the act requires financial institutions to keep records of cash payments and file reports of cash purchases or negotiable instruments of more than $10,000 as a daily aggregate amount. Of course, this is all sold as a way of tracking criminals.

The US government employs other means of making war on cash also. Up until 1945, there were 500 dollar bills, 1,000 dollar bills, and 10,000 dollar bills in circulation. There was even a 100,000 dollar bill in the 1930s with which banks made clearings between one another. The US government stopped issuing these bills in 1945 and by 1969 had withdrawn all from circulation. So, in the guise of fighting organized crime and money laundering, what's actually occurred is that they made it very inconvenient to use cash. A one hundred dollar bill today has $15.50 worth of purchasing power in 1969 dollars, when they removed the last big bills.

The Problem Is International

The war on cash in Sweden has gone probably the furthest and Scandinavian governments in general are notable for their opposition to cash. In Swedish cities, tickets for public buses no longer can be purchased for cash; they must be purchased in advance by a cell phone or text message—in other words, via bank accounts.

The deputy governor of the Swedish Central Bank gloated, before his retirement a few years back, that cash will survive "like the crocodile," even though it may be forced to see its habitat gradually cut back.

The analogy is apt since three of the four major Swedish banks combined have more than two-thirds of their offices no longer accepting or paying out cash. These three banks want to phase out the manual handling of cash at their offices at a very rapid pace and have been doing that since 2012.

In France, opponents of cash tried to pass a law in 2012 which would restrict the use of cash from a maximum of 3,000 euros per exchange to 1,000. The law failed, but then there was the attack on Charlie Hebdo and on a Jewish supermarket, so immediately the state used this as a reason for getting the 1,000 maximum limit. They got their maximum limit. Why? Well, proponents claim that these attacks were partially financed by cash.

The terrorists used cash to purchase some of the stuff they needed. No doubt, these murderers also wore shoes and clothing and used cell phones and cars during the planning and execution of their mayhem. Why not ban these things? A naked barefoot terrorist without communications is surely less effective than the fully clothed and equipped one.

Finally, Switzerland, formerly a great bastion of economic liberty and financial privacy, has succumbed under the bareknuckle tactics of the US government. The Swiss government has banned all cash payments of more than 100,000 francs (about $106,000), including transactions involving watches, real estate, precious metals, and cars. This was done under the threat of blacklisting by the Organization of Economic Development, with the US no doubt pushing behind the scenes. Transactions above 100,000 francs will now have to be processed through the banking system. The reason is to prevent the catch-all crime, of course, of money laundering.

Chase Bank has also recently joined the war on cash. It's the largest bank in the US, a subsidiary of JP Morgan Chase and Co., and according to Forbes, the world's third largest public company. It also received $25 billion in bailout loans from the US Treasury. As of March, Chase began restricting the use of cash in selected markets. The new policy restricts borrowers from using cash to make payments on credit cards, mortgages, equity lines, and auto loans.

Chase even goes as far as to prohibit the storage of cash in its safe deposit boxes. In a letter to its customers, dated April 1, 2015, pertaining to its "updated safe deposit box lease agreement," one of the high-lighted items reads, "You agree not to store any cash or coins other than those found to have a collectible value." Whether or not this pertains to gold and silver coins with no collectible value is not explained, but of course it does. As one observer warned, "This policy is unusual, but since Chase is the nation's largest bank, I wouldn't be surprised if we start seeing more of this in this era of sensitivity about funding terrorists and other illegal causes." So, get your money out of those safe deposit boxes, your currency and probably your gold and silver.

Only (Supervised) Spending is Allowed

Gregory Mankiw, a prominent macroeconomist, came up with a scheme in 2009: the Fed would announce that a year from the date of the announcement, it intended to pick a numeral from 0 to 9 out of a hat. All currency with a serial number ending in that numeral, would instantly lose status as legal tender, causing the expected return on holding currency to plummet to -10 percent. This would allow the Fed to reduce interest rates below zero for a year or even more because people would happily loan money for say, -2 percent or -4 percent because that would stop them from losing 10 percent.

Now the reason given by our rulers for suppressing cash is to keep society safe from terrorists, tax evaders, money launderers, drug cartels, and other villains real or imagined. The actual aim of the flood of laws restricting or even prohibiting the use of cash is to force the public to make payments through the financial system. This enables governments to expand their ability to spy on and keep track of their citizens' most private financial dealings, in order to milk their citizens of every last dollar of tax payments that they claim are due.

Other reasons for suppressing cash are (1) to prop up the unstable fractional reserve banking system, which is in a state of collapse all over the world, and (2) to give central banks the power to impose negative nominal interest rates. That is, to make you spend money by subtracting money from your bank account for every day you leave it in the bank account and don't spend it.

The Failed Economics
of "Neoliberalism"

16

What's the Difference Between Liberalism and "Neoliberalism"?

by Ryan McMaken

It is possible that there is no term more abused in modern political discourse than "liberalism." Originally meant to describe the ideology of free trade and limited government, the anti-capitalist left adopted the term in the 1930s and changed its meaning to the opposite of what it meant in the nineteenth century.

Liberalism never quite lost its correct meaning in most of the world, however, and in Spanish-speaking countries, for example, the word "liberalismo" still often means the ideology of free trade and free markets. Only American right-wingers appear to use the term as a pejorative to sling at the anti-capitalist left. Even in America, though, with the left having eschewed the term for the more trendy "progressive," the use of "liberalism" in political invective appears to be fading.

Ryan McMaken, "What's the Difference Between Liberalism and 'Neoliberalism'?" *Mises Wire* (October 21, 2016).

As if this weren't complicated enough, liberalism has now been saddled once again with a new variation, the meaning of which remains unclear: "neoliberalism."

What is neoliberalism? Well, it appears that, at least among its critics, "neoliberalism" usually means nothing more than "liberalism."

"Neoliberalism" As a Pejorative Term for *Laissez-Faire* Liberalism

To get a sense of the common usage for a term, it never hurts to check Wikipedia, and in this case, we find that neoliberalism is simply liberalism:

> Neoliberalism is a controversial term that refers primarily to the 20th century resurgence of 19th century ideas associated with *laissez-faire* economic liberalism. These include extensive economic liberalization policies such as privatization, fiscal austerity, deregulation, free trade, and reductions in government spending in order to enhance the role of the private sector in the economy.

But why is it a controversial term? The controversy stems from the fact that the term is primarily used as a pejorative term and not as a good-faith descriptive term to denote an ideology.

In a study of 148 articles on political economy that use the term, authors Taylor Boas and Jordan Gans-Morse found that the term "neoliberalism" is almost never used in a positive light. The study found that 45 percent of the time, the term is used in a neutral fashion, but 45 percent of the time, is it used to portray liberalism negatively. Only 3 percent of the time is the term used in a way designed to cast free markets in a positive light.

In other words, "neoliberalism" is really just an anti-liberal slogan.

Boas and Gans-Morse continue:

One compelling indicator of the term's negative connotation is that virtually *no one* self-identifies as a neoliberal, even though scholars frequently associate others—politicians, economic advisors, and even fellow academics—with this term. While a fifth of the articles on neoliberalism in our sample referred prominently to other people as neoliberals, in all of our research, we did not uncover a single contemporary instance in which an author used the term self-descriptively ...

Moreover, as Boas and Gans-Morse note, "neoliberalism" is often used to "denote...a radical, far-reaching application of free-market economics unprecedented in speed, scope, or ambition." For those wishing to appear "reasonable" or nonradical, neoliberalism's connotations as being radically in favor of free markets provide an additional reason to avoid self-identifying with the term.

This unwillingness to self-identify extends to mises.org, although not for reasons of avoiding radicalism. As editor, I have published more than one article here that makes distinctions between the liberalism of the Austrian school and the so-called neoliberals. Philipp Bagus's review essay, "Why Austrians Are Not Neoliberals" explains many of these distinctions in detail. In another article, Guido Hülsmann describes Ludwig von Mises's own battle against an early group of neoliberals at the Mont Pelerin Society. In Mises's eyes, these neoliberals were *relatively* liberal—compared to doctrinaire socialists—but were interventionists who favored central banking and the bureaucratic, regulatory state. Then as now, the central problem with the neoliberals revolved around their blithe attitude toward inherently anti-market central banks and government-created money.

To those of us who keep up with the details of the market-place in liberal ideas, these distinctions are readily apparent.

To anti-liberal leftists looking in from the outside, how-ever, Austrians, Chicagoans, and neo-classicals all probably look like pretty much the same thing. These "neoliberals" all say nice things about markets and free trade, so they all must agree with those neoliberals at the International Monetary Fund. Or so it is assumed. After all, don't we hear from the IMF about the importance of free trade and balanced budgets and limiting government spending? The fact that the IMF sup-ports central banking, bank bailouts, and corporatist deals for the politically-connected is lost on those who only see the IMF's *ostensible* support for markets. The anti-liberals then lump together IMF President Christine Lagarde and Ludwig von Mises.

In the UK, for example, it's easy to find articles that equate neoliberalism with the alleged free-market policies of Ronald Reagan and Margaret Thatcher. In this article at *The Guard-ian*, for example, George Monbiot views Thatcherism and Rea-ganism as the vanguards of a supposed hard-core free-market hegemony we groan under today.

The Anti-Neoliberalism Movement Is Just an Anti-Capitalist Movement

Naomi Klein, a perennial critic of neoliberalism, sees the pop-ularity of the Bernie Sanders movement as a defeat for neolib-eralism. In a recent radio interview, she stated:

So neoliberalism lost the argument. They lost the argu-ment, to the extent that not only was Bernie out there calling himself a socialist, not apologizing for it, mak-ing these arguments that, you know, we—not reduc-tions in tuition, but free college, you know, just pushing the envelope, 100 percent renewables, just going all the way, and people were cheering. And he forced Hillary Clinton to move to the left. And we also saw that even Donald Trump had to throw out the rule—the neoliberal rule book, trashed free trade agreements, promised to defend the social safety net, in order to build his base.

In other words, in Klein's mind, a victory against neoliberalism brings with it hard-left environmentalism, opposition to free trade, "free college," and "mov[ing] to the left" in general.

Not surprisingly, sometimes Klein and other opponents of neoliberalism are right *by accident*. They often (correctly) oppose trade deals like the TPP, for example. But, they do so for the wrong reasons. They oppose these trade agreements not because they are extensions of the regulatory, corporatist state, but because the anti-liberals mistakenly view these trade deals as being for actual free trade and free markets.

Opposing Both the Neoliberals and the Anti-Liberals

The conclusion we're forced to draw is that consistent advocates for *laissez-faire* are stuck between both the actual neoliberals (as identified by Mises) and the anti-capitalist, antineoliberal left. If they could, the anti-neoliberals such as Klein and Sanders would happily expropriate and nationalize entire industries. Entrepreneurship would wither, small business would be regulated out of business, and the financial sector would function—even more than it already does—as a *de facto* state-owned enterprise.

Meanwhile, the neoliberals found at the IMF and central banks of the world continue to manipulate the global economy through monetary policy, bail out favored cronies at major corporations, and support corporatist policies in general.

Both groups continue to present significant threats to the cause of *laissez faire*.

17

How Today's Central Bankers Threaten Civilization

by Claudio Grass

When I was asked to write an article about the impact of negative interest rates and negative yielding bonds, I thought it was a chance to look at the topic from a broader perspective. There have been lots of articles speculating about the possible implications and focusing on their impact in the short run, but it's not very often that an analysis looks a bit further into the future, trying to connect money and its effect on society itself.

Qui Bono?

Let us begin with a basic question, that lies at the heart of this issue: Who profits from a loan that is guaranteed to pay back less than the amount borrowed? Obviously, it is the borrower and not the lender, which in our case is the government and those closely connected to it. Negative rates and negative-yielding bonds by definition favor the debtors and punish the

Gladio Grass, "How Today's Central Bankers Threaten Civilization," *Mises Wire* (December 23, 2019). Originally published at executive-global.com.

savers. In addition, these policies are an affront to basic economic principles and to common sense too. They contradict all logical ideas about how money works and they have no basis and no precedent in any organic economic system. Thus, now, in addition to the hidden tax that is inflation, we also have another mechanism that redistributes wealth from the average citizen to those at the top of the pyramid.

Thus, this very concept of a central authority being able to bend and twist the rules, even when the result is illogical, has implications that extend way beyond daily economic activities. In fact, it ultimately divides society into two classes, those who profit from this arbitrary and unilateral rewriting of the rules and those who are forced to pay the price even though they never agreed to it. In fact, they weren't even asked.

A System of Collective Corruption

Of course, we can also look at it from the collective perspective of the so-called social contract of Rousseau and argue that this system of overt (taxation) and covert (monetary policy) redistribution is legitimate, or even benign. You might still believe that the state will take care of you in the future, and thus you are willing to sacrifice a part of your wealth and savings today to make sure that happens. In that case, it is useful to remember that the current central banking system is not that old. It's only been around for about hundred years, or two long-term debt cycles combined. The first cycle ended when President Nixon officially tried to demonetize gold in 1971, empowering a centralized system whereby a few decide who receives the currency first and at what interest rate, allowing them to create bubbles in certain asset classes, protect different key industries and to use it to finance wars and enrich politicians and those close to them.

So far, total credit on a global scale stands around $240 trillion. It's hard to conceive of such a number, but if you consider that 1 trillion seconds are equal to 31,709 years, you might begin to wrap your head around just how leveraged the system has become. We should never forget that debt is always consumption brought forward. That being said, debts need to be paid back or forgiven—there is no other outcome. In addition, the amount of debt that a system can take on is limited, and when a credit-based system can't grow any further, the logical outcome is the collapse of the whole system. As Ludwig von Mises described this a long time ago,

> There is no means of avoiding the final collapse of a boom brought about by credit expansion. The alternative is only whether the crisis should come sooner as the result of a voluntary abandonment of further credit expansion, or later as a final and total catastrophe of the currency system involved.

This is the reason why central banks started trying to avoid this systemic collapse by taking interest rates below zero and allowing the big players to take on debt for free and to reduce their debt burden at the same time. This, of course, is something that we already witnessed extensively during the past decade and it is just a matter of time until more central banks, including the Federal Reserve, use the same fraudulent tactic to let some air out of the balloon, and to deleverage the debtor at the cost of the saver. However, it is very questionable whether this can be successfully managed, especially since demographics have been a problem for decades in the West, making growth a problem too. Governments enforced a mass-immigration policy to fight this aging population trend, yet its execution has been disastrous; instead of rejuvenating nations and spurring productivity, it has ended up crushing the national welfare systems.

It is thus clear that the current path that governments and central bankers have selected is utterly unsustainable and that their attempts at short-term "patches" have little hope of stopping the inevitable implosion, which has already been decades in the making. Pretending otherwise is as futile as it is naïve. As Ayn Rand put it,

> We can ignore reality, but we cannot ignore the consequences of ignoring reality.

The "De-Civilization" Effect

Negative interest rates are a great example of these short-term patches, only in this case, they are not just useless as a cure for our economic ills, but they actually do more harm than good.

The outcome of this policy is that time becomes worthless. As one's hard-earned money, set aside for a rainy day or for one's children's education, instead of appreciating, as logic would dictate, diminishes day by day, it does not make sense any longer to produce and to save. The basic motivation for each individual to get up in the morning and to work hard to achieve a higher living standard is removed, and time, therefore, turns into a dimension without any value. If people can't save any longer, by government decree, then there is no other way than to consume. And with all traditionally safe investment options gone, they are only left with the option of speculating in rigged financial markets, and the massive risk that comes with it, especially now, when we're nearing the end of a long-term debt cycle.

The individual is thus turned more and more into a state dependent, as the basis for a free life is financial independence and the ability have savings on the side that keep you self-reliant. The fundament of a successful system requires individuals that live a decent life, knowing that they must first produce before they can consume.

The masses are trained and forced to consume and spend money they don't have to buy things they don't need. Our monetary system in combination with this kind of public policy causes mass overconsumption, the destruction of wealth, capital consumption, and the destruction and exploitation of nature.

People significantly add value to society if they are able to save, as this allows them to invest at a later stage, once they have accumulated as much as needed, and thereby aid others in their own efforts to succeed and to reach financial independence. Parents can help their children and investors can help budding new companies that bring innovative ideas that benefit the economy and society as a whole. As this virtuous cycle continues, based on productivity, long-term thinking, and responsible financial management, "the rising tide lift all boats."

To the contrary, when this natural process is forcibly disrupted and reversed, the effects are deleterious and far-reaching: mass overconsumption, the destruction of wealth, and the exploitation of nature and the environment are all symptoms of this institutional and massive push towards short-term thinking and of being forced to focus just on today, at the expense of tomorrow.

Wider Implications

Thus, what is at stake is not only the world economy, but the accelerating decline of Western culture, which, based on liberalism (personal freedom and private property rights) and Christianity (personal responsibility), laid the foundation for a decentralized Europe that allowed for competition of goods and services but especially the competition of ideas.

This dangerous decline is nothing new, either, as it began after World War I, when Europe turned towards a more centralized approach, with all sorts of collectivist ideas causing all kinds of schisms that we still see today in modern societies. Today, we see a rapid acceleration of this decline, as our economic system can barely remain standing, and as our politics and our societies devolve even faster into tribal or more precisely into political identity groups, fighting each other over meaningless feuds. All the while they are distracted from the real threat, the one that governments and central banks pose to their future and to their children's future.

As long as people are afraid of liberty and falsely delegate their self-responsibility to a central authority, hope is dim. It's time to think independently about whether today's centralized system really makes sense, if it is sustainable, and for how much longer. If the answers to these questions scare you, it is pointless to expect solutions to come from above. It is then time to act directly and responsibly, with a solid plan, hard physical assets privately owned, and a long-term strategy that does not depend on the whims and caprices of those in charge.

18

What Would Mises Think about the West Today?

by Jeff Deist

Introduction

Those of us who read and enjoy Mises, and he wrote so much about so many things, might well wonder what he would have to say about the state of America and the West in 2019. After all, he was a sociologist and philosopher and political theorist as well as an economist. Surely we could use his perspective today, and so much of what he wrote was prescient and still relevant.

Of course It is always dangerous to imagine what any departed intellectual or thinker would think about today's world and today's events, and this is certainly true of Mises too. We all love to do this, though. We all want to use Mises to make our points about topic X, Y, or Z today, to confirm our own biases or bolster our arguments—and why not? I'm always mystified by facile objections to "appeal to authority"—I recognize Mises

Jeff Deist, "What Would Mises Think about the West Today?" This is an excerpt from a talk given at the Mises Institute's Supports Summit in Los Angeles, October 27, 2019.

may in fact be wrong, and you, Mr. Arguer on Facebook, may in fact be right. But I doubt it.

Two problems present themselves. First, we know how difficult it is to compare eras in sports. How do we measure Babe Ruth and Mickey Mantle against Barry Bonds or Mike Trout? Mises was a man of Old Europe, born before the Great War and the fall of the Habsburgs. Even the world of New York in 1973 when he died is a long way from Woke America 2019.

Second, if we think of scholars like artists or musicians, how do we weigh their work as a whole? Do we accord more weight to his later work, representing a more developed world-view? Or do we approach his work like a rock band, where *The Theory of Money and Credit* was his promising freshman album and *Human Action* was his best and biggest seller? What were his greatest hits?

It's a very fraught question, considering his bibliography consists of nearly twenty full length books, hundreds of articles and monographs, and millions of words written over nearly six decades. It's daunting to draw simple conclusions from such a varied body of work because people change over time. And of course while brilliant and prolific thinkers should be read as authorities, as Mises certainly was regarding socialism, no mortal has the dispositive last word on any issue or topic.

But of course we should apply Mises's counsel to the world today. After all, what's the point of learning from him? He's someone you can spend a lifetime reading and learning from, someone whose work never feels dated or irrelevant. He is someone we still have to grapple with.

So we do wonder what Mises might think about all kinds of things, like the Nobel prize his protege Hayek won just after Mises's death. Or about Austria today, a shadow of its late nineteenth century glory. Or the collapse of the Soviet Union and the Eastern Bloc. Or about the European project, especially the Eurozone, the creation of the ECB, and the Euro itself, and the political state of Europe today. About European immigration and the Schengen Agreement. About negative interest rates and QE and crazed central bank policies in the decades since his death. About business cycles busts in 1987 and 2000 and 2008. About gold and cryptocurrency. About Trump and the current crop of Democrats, and Brexit and Merkel and Mario Draghi. About democracy as a mechanism for peaceful transfers of political power. About renewed calls for socialism in the west. About the state of Austrian school economics. And we might especially wonder about what Mises would think about the current state of the liberal project he laid out one hundred years ago.

Mises the Neoliberal?

Is Misesean liberalism in retreat across the West, or has it triumphed? I suspect he would be shocked to discover he is now viewed as a central figure today's dominant ideology of neoliberalism, which we are assured has taken over everything. It's an ersatz form of liberalism, certainly, that nobody has a precise definition for. But we might take a stab at it:

Neoliberalism is loosely the basic program of late twentieth century western governments (social democracy, public education, civil rights, entitlements, welfare, feminism, LGBT rights, and a degree of global governance by supra-national organizations), coupled with at least grudging respect for the role of markets in improving human life. This vision of course includes western interventionism (military, diplomatic, and economic) in all world affairs, led always by the US. Neoliberals are left-liberals who accept the role of markets and the need for economic development as part of the larger liberal program, coupled with unwavering belief in neoconservative foreign policy. Think U2's Bono, or Hillary Clinton.

In other words, neoliberalism is a mixed bag. Property—what Mises considered the distillation of the entire liberal program—certainly is not the animating force in the neoliberal world. But let us not gloss over the tepid acknowledgement by neoliberals that markets work. This was in no way established in the first half of the twentieth century, when western academics told us socialism was scientific and inevitable. This alone is a huge achievement—and who in the twentieth century did more to make the case for markets than Mises?

Even a cursory search of the *New York Times* and *Washington Post*—someone would have to show him how to Google this—reveals his name mentioned in dozens and dozens of articles just since 2015. These mentions usually come in the context of how economists took over politics, and thus public policy is completely captured by free-market radicals who got their crazy ideas from Mises. Just this year a University of Alabama history professor published a book titled *The Marginal Revolutionaries: How Austrian Economists Fought the War of Ideas* which is a leftwing homage to the continuing influence of the Austrian school among the (supposedly) anti-socialist upper echelons of business and government—with Mises as its leader.

Mises, as much as Hayek, is now one of the Left's favorite avatars for market liberalism. His name is far better known today, and his work far more widely read today, than it ever was during his lifetime. What more could any intellectual hope for? And most of the big names in economics who dominated the twentieth century, men like Arthur Burns who enjoyed comfortable positions at Columbia and later chaired the Fed, are footnotes today. Mises's name and legacy, by contrast, have been elevated. Even his worst critics now see him not only as a giant not only of economics, but a hugely influential figure in western capitalism. This was not the case when he died in 1973.

The Health of Austrian Economics

Mises's posthumous renaissance reflects an upswing in the broader fortunes of Austrian economics generally. It's easy to look at the central bankers of the world and think economics is hopelessly lost, but this would miss a very strong subcurrent in the profession.

A few years ago Professor Walter Block had an email exchange with the late Dr. Gary Becker, the Nobel Prize winner at the University of Chicago. Block, a former student of Becker, lamented the treatment of Austrian scholars in certain academic journals. In response, Becker argued that much of what is good and groundbreaking in Austrian theory already has been incorporated into mainstream economics.

Becker reminded Walter that Austrians already made huge advancements by explaining the impossibility of socialist calculation, presenting a theory of entrepreneurship, and pioneering the role of time in capital and interest theory. All of this came from such a famous economist who viewed the Austrian school from an impartial and somewhat skeptical vantage point. Becker did not mention, though he hardly needed to, how the earthquake known as the Marginal Revolution was in good part Mengerian. The point is that we often underestimate the impact Austrians have had on both economics and society. It's baked into the modern cake, so to speak, so we take it for granted.

Imagine Mises's reaction to having virtually every important Austrian treatise, book, paper, and article available free and instantly online, often translated into multiple languages. Imagine his reaction to the number of Austrian and Austrian-friendly professors teaching in economics departments and business schools across the world. And imagine his reaction to organizations like the Mises Institute dedicated to advancing his work. Certainly the Austrian school is in far better shape today than he could have imagined, even with the degradation of academia.

That's not to say he would think very highly of economics generally today. He might wonder why people like Thomas Piketty, Paul Krugman, Binaymin Appelbaum, and Noah Smith at *Bloomberg* are viewed as economists at all, given their lack of substantive work. He would lament the hyperspecialization of economists, none of whom are faintly equipped to write treatises. He certainly would be dismayed by the abandonment of theoretical work for mathematical and statistical modeling, and the conflation of trendy disciplines like behavioral economics with real academic work.

Central Banks and Money

What about monetary economics? I suspect he would be amazed by the sheer force of central bank money creation in the 1980s, 1990s, 2000s, and 2010s. He didn't live to see Paul Volcker's Fed Funds Rate of 20 percent, and he undoubtedly would view today's near-zero and negative central banks rates as un-economic forms of monetary alchemy, a central bankers' version of animal spirits. Undoubtedly he would see figures like Greenspan, Bernanke, and Draghi as untethered radicals who made things up as they went along. He would not see programs like quantitative easing as banking at all, but purely as political machinations.

Ours would not be a rational central bank world to Mises, who perhaps never foresaw how long fiat currencies could operate as political money—if powerful enough governments back them up. I also suspect he would see the business cycle theory he helped develop has not been further developed by economists who recognize its broad brush strokes as correct but lacking in detail. Yes, inflation is a monetary phenomenon, and yes central banks create cycles of malinvestment, boom, and bust—but understanding the timing and duration is where I think Mises would want Austrians to focus today.

Academia and Socialism

But beyond economics and banking he might be appalled to see how universities in general have become what he termed "nurseries of socialism" even more today than in his time. Because today socialists don't organize in union halls or loading docks, they organize in university sociology departments. The working class failed them, so today they've turned to woke intersectional academics as the vanguard. The animating spirit of Bernie and Elizabeth Warren and Antifa lives on campus, and I think Mises would deplore this very much. I think he would especially shake his head at the rising amount of support for socialism among young people, nearly one hundred years after he wrote the definitive case against it, and against the backdrop of the twentieth century's collectivist failures. Surely it would be hard for someone who believed so strongly in using arguments instead of bullets to see the West today backsliding politically toward collectivism and bloodshed.

Immigration and Nationalism

Regarding immigration and the aforementioned Schengen Agreement, Mises might well wonder what the fuss is all about. Lew Rockwell points out how in Mises's young life a businessman could take a train from Vienna to London and disembark without ever showing or needing a passport. But of course early 1900s Austria was a very different time and place, before two world wars with all their dislocations, mass immigration into and across Europe, and centralized bureaucratic welfare states.

We can say with certainty he worried about the idea of polyglot countries and the plight of ethnic or linguistic minorities. That is precisely why both *Liberalism* and *Nation, State, and Economy* were radically decentralist in their approach, making the case for a liberal nationalism rooted property, self-determination, and *laissez-faire* at home; peaceful nonintervention abroad; and free flowing international trade to deter the bellicose expansionism of autarky.

Our world today is not exactly full of Misesean liberal states; obviously the opposite is true. And in fact Mises was concerned about migration into illiberal states, where recent arrivals seek to change existing institutions for the worse. But don't take my word for it: Professor Ben Powell of Texas Tech University, himself a vocal advocate for completely open borders, recently wrote a paper titled "Solving the Misesean Migration Conundrum."

Quoting Powell:

The problem, for Mises, lies in the fact that states, in his time and ours, are not liberal. They are interventionist. Once states interfere with economic activity, some people are able to use the state to secure economic gains for themselves at the expense of others living under that same government. Once different nations are living under the same government, they come into conflict with each or, as Mises put it, "Migrations thus bring members of some nations into the territories of other nations. That gives rise to particularly characteristic conflicts between people."

However, the institutions of freedom are not exogenously given. Among other factors, they depend on the ideology, political beliefs, and culture of the population controlling the state. Immigrants often migrate from origin countries with dysfunctional institutional environments that lack economic freedom. If the immigrants' own belief system, was, in part, responsible for that dysfunctional system, and they bring those beliefs with them to the destination country in too great of numbers, too rapidly, to assimilate to the beliefs in the destination country, they could erode the very institutions responsible for the high productivity that attracted them in the first place. Thus, immigration itself could, in principle, turn a relatively free destination country, where Mises wouldn't see immigrants as a problem, into a more interventionist state where immigration does create the problems Mises fears.

So while Mises certainly understood migration restrictions just as surely as he understood trade restrictions, it's an outright mistake and not just an oversimplification to insist he would unequivocally support open borders in Europe today.

Conclusion

There is so much more to say about what Mises would tell us today. Most of all I know he would be thrilled by this event happening today, in his honor. Of course he knew Lew Rockwell from their Arlington House days, but he never imagined a Mises Institute. He never imagined a university in the American South would become a haven for studying his work and the broader Austrian school. He never imagined a digital world which would make much of his writing, his life's work, available online to anyone around the world, almost instantaneously and free of charge. And as mentioned, he never imagined his work would be more widely read, that he would be more famous, after his death.

Yes, liberalism—the good and true version, has unraveled. It didn't hold. We shouldn't lie about this, or pretend it hasn't happened. The West is politically illiberal today, and getting worse. But that does not counsel despair. Whether we are gaining or losing ground, whether we are winning or losing, is a matter of perspective. Mises sometimes succumbed to pessimism, as evidenced by his memoirs. Anyone who lived through the Great War, who had to flee authoritarianism twice, can be excused for this. We don't have that excuse. We have the full body of Mises's work to read and enjoy, to guide us in our thoughts and actions today. And we should share his sense of *élan vital*, what he called the "ineradicable craving" that compels us to seek happiness, minimize discontent, and spend our lives "*purposively* struggling against the forces adverse to (us)."

What would Mises think of this gathering today, in this room? I think he would be thrilled to know, seventy-five years after speaking here, that an audience of people still find his ideas captivating and worth considering.

19

Mises and the "New Economics"

by Jeff Deist

I. Introduction

What a wonderful gathering of students today, on this impressive and beautiful campus. We can see why Hans Sennholz loved this place, and why Drs. Herbener and Ritenour so enjoy living and teaching here. You are all too young to serve as the "remnant," so we will consider you the vanguard instead. I'm always impressed by young people with an interest in serious scholarship and ideas, who have the intellect to read 900-page books. We are told nobody reads anymore, and certainly not dense tomes about economic theory, but this raises a question: are the rare people who do read such books likely to be more important or less important in the future? I suspect the former.

Imagine how pleased Ludwig von Mises would be by this conference today, to know people still find his work vital and relevant nearly half a century after his death. He is far better

---

This article is excerpted from a talk delivered on February 22, 2020 at the Austrian Student Scholars Conference, hosted by Grove City College in Pennsylvania.

known today, and far more widely read, than during his lifetime. And most of his important works today are available in multiple languages, online, free and instantly to anyone around the world. What more could any important thinker want?

There is a wonderful French expression, *élan vital*, which technically translates to "vital impulse" or "vital force" in English. The early twentieth-century French philosopher Henri Bergson developed the term to describe the creative force within an organism which drives growth, change, and desirable adaptation. Professor Mises liked it so much that he discussed it toward the end of *Human Action*, to make the broader point that human history is not deterministic, that individuals acting purposefully and willfully could change their fortunes. In other words, human volition trumps fate. We are all possessed of at least some measure of our own *élan vital*.

Now for some reason, dead philosophers get a lot more respect than dead economists! Maybe this is because philosophy seems ancient and timeless, suited to the human experience across any age.

II. Dead Economists vs. Presentism

But if Bergson's vital force moves us inexorably forward, why study dead economists at all? What can an economist like Mises, born in the late nineteenth century into a vastly different world, teach us today? Why in the world should a group of young students gather in Grove City, Pennsylvania, in 2020, to consider a school of economics with roots in Habsburg-era Vienna?

These are fair questions, given the relentless doctrine of "presentism" which dominates everything in our culture today. Presentism is the ahistorical and arrogant insistence on interpreting past events, historical figures, and existing bodies of knowledge by the supposedly enlightened standard of our time—standards which shift so rapidly that today's wokest enforcers are tomorrow's victims of the mob.

Presentism is at the core of the progressive worldview, which insists the past is always retrograde, the present is always better but still deeply imperfect, and the future has an ultimately happy deterministic arc. It is one manifestation of the hubris which comes from imagining we live in a unique time, and a uniquely enlightened time.

Presentism is the hallmark of the imagined economics smart set: the Paul Krugmans, Christine Lagardes, Thomas Pikettys, Noah Smiths, and Benyamin Appelbaums of today. The economics they advocate—mostly in blogs, social media, financial news shows, or pop books, and never in treatises—is *sui generis*, unique to them. It's their own economics, created out of whole cloth by them individually, supposedly scientific and brand new, to suit today's world. It's a New Economics for 2020. And of course they all insist they're merely following and interpreting the data, going where it takes them. After all, they're scientists!

But exactly what theory or education or discipline do they apply to that data? Is it really economics?

Of course we know there is no New Economics any more than there is new physics or new calculus. There are *advances* and *discoveries* in economic science, and there are new technologies which of course have an enormous effect on economies. But economics is, and always will be, about human action in the context of choice, scarcity, opportunity cost, and subjective measures of value.

It's no secret where these economists and professors and *New York Times* pundits get their views, even if they don't have much of a sense of their place in the field. And why should they? It's entirely possible to obtain a PhD in economics without taking a single course in the history of economic thought. Their economics represent warmed-over Marx, or Keynes, or

John Kenneth Galbraith, or Paul Samuelson, though they rarely mention these names. They don't announce themselves as neo-Keynesians, or Samuelsonites, or as advancing the views of any dead economist—because presentism makes that unthinkable. They are their own economists!

But it turns out their ideas and policy ideas aren't new at all. It's all about demand, demand, demand, whether from workers or shoppers or homebuyers or restaurant diners or students paying $40,000 for a year of college. Every economic policy they conjure, whether fiscal or monetary, comes down to one goal: stimulating demand, encouraging all of us to want to borrow more and spend more. That's it. All of their modern economic theories come down to consumption *über alles*. That's how the modern profession thinks we create an economy.

Austrian economists, by contrast, often tend to preface every argument with a reference back to the old masters like Mises or Hayek, as though there is only old economics. It's a marketing problem in a world of presentism! Are modern Austrians simply less egotistical than their peers, and thus attempt to provide support and foundation for their work? Do they simply recognize economics is built on an edifice of previous knowledge which can't be thrown out with the bathwater at every new crisis?

But this goes against the grain, because "everybody knows" those old Austrian theories no longer apply in our digital age. Hubris is the order of our day, not the humility of a cautious and circumspect social scientist engaged in truth seeking.

III. How Economics Lost Its Way

So why indeed should we consider dead economists? The answer, of course, is that they still have something to tell us about the world and how it works, that their work forms the foundation from which today's analysis should begin. Something the Krugmans and Pikettys, always shooting from the hip and following the data wherever it goes, cannot provide.

In fact, from what I can tell most economists don't concern themselves much at all with finding truth or helping us better understand the world. Their focus is not on serving humanity by working to increase our wealth and happiness. From my perspective economics exists mostly to provide sinecures for people whose chief concern is whether a tiny group of their peers think they're smart.

Somewhere along the way, economics stopped attempting to serve humanity by making us happier, healthier, and wealthier. Somewhere along the way, economics became a discipline of hyperspecialized technicians, of statistics and data and models. Somewhere along the way, economics got small. It lost its *élan vital*.

So what happened? In a sense economics simply succumbed to the ugly hubris of our day.

The mood in the West is not friendly to intellectuals, much less dead intellectuals. We prefer social media and short videos to books and lectures. We want journalism to provide entertainment, to match our short attention spans. We want someone to curate and provide us with easily digestible information and news, rather than seeking original sources for ourselves. We don't have time for context or nuance. With limited knowledge of history, we tend to fetishize new over old, modernity over tradition, and data over theory. In our self-regard we imagine ourselves in a new era, where old knowledge and wisdom no longer apply.

But we imagine this at our own peril. The accelerating pace of technology lulls us into believing human development is linear. Technology, not dusty old ideas from another century, seems the primary driver of change. But technology can't answer the age-old question of whether humans choose compulsion or cooperation: it cannot create a "third way" between market and state. Ideas still rule the world, but sometimes we mistake new technology for new ideas.

All of the exciting developments seem to abound only in the physical sciences. Quantum mechanics promises to dramatically increase computing power. Physicists and engineers make the possibility of affordable private space travel closer to reality every day. Advances in artificial intelligence, computer science, and information technology promise to radically alter our physical world through an emerging Internet of Things. If there's one thing that still excites the Western imagination, it is the possibility of radical advances in technology—all due, at least in large part, to advances and applications in the physical sciences.

By contrast, the social sciences and humanities are moribund, reduced to hyphenated studies and manufactured "intersectionality" disciplines. Academic work in the soft sciences is shrill and brittle, far more concerned with political and cultural crusades than teaching students or engaging in serious scholarship. Music, cinema, modern art, and literature suffer under the weight of their own pretensions and heavy-handed messaging. Historians whitewash history, English professors ignore English literature, and sociology devolves into a definitional science. Yale scraps art history.

Then we have economics, the orphaned social science whose practitioners masquerade as data miners. Economics has become the unwitting younger cousin to math, statistics, and finance, which explains why so many universities have shunted it off onto their business schools. Empiricism, the jealous impulse to apply scientific methodology to problems of human action, insists that economists have value only to the extent that they successfully test and "prove" their hypotheses.

As a result, economics has been corrupted into a predictive discipline which fails to correctly predict anything; into a prescriptive discipline which prescribes the wrong policies;

and into an empirical discipline which collects data but misses the point.

IV. Why We Need Mises

This is exactly why we need Mises, who perhaps more than any economist of his time understood economics as a theoretical science. But readers of Mises appreciate not only the depth and breadth of his insights, but also the elegance of his language. Even writing in English, a language he adopted in middle age, Mises conveyed dense conceptual theories and big ideas with a vigorous style not normally associated with economists. Nothing in his writing is dry or technical. This is why, for example, opening *Human Action* to any random page can yield immediate benefits. To use an analogy from the days when music came on vinyl and compact discs, with songs in a particular order, there are no throwaway songs in Mises's work.

Mises did not hesitate to borrow heavily from other fields in his writing, including history, sociology, and philosophy (especially epistemology and logic), always in the service of presenting economics holistically. His drive to understand the broader implications of human action and reason saved him from the kind of tunnel vision we see in academia today, where intersectionality—far from what its trendy name suggests—serves a narrow political purpose rather than the broader cause of advancing knowledge.

In this sense he demonstrated a characteristic humility, contrasted with the hubris displayed by so many brilliant academics: he understood his chosen profession as part of a larger human experience, rather than a self-serving body of knowledge with rigid boundaries to be guarded even as they continually bump up against other disciplines.

One great example of Mises's wonderful use of language comes at the end of *Human Action*, in a typically ambitious chapter titled "Economics and the Essential Problems of Human Existence." As usual, Mises's syntax and diction hardly bring to mind a boring economics text:

> Our "ineradicable craving" compels us to seek happiness, minimize discontent, and spend our lives "purposively struggling against the forces adverse to (us)."
>
> "Civilization, it is said, makes people poorer, because it multiplies their wishes and does not soothe, but kindles, desires. All the busy doings and dealings of hardworking men, their hurrying, pushing, and bustling are nonsensical, for they provide neither happiness nor quiet.
>
> Yet all such qualms, doubts, and scruples are subdued by the irresistible force of man's vital energy. As long as a man lives, he cannot help obeying the cardinal impulse, the *élan vital.*"

Not the kind of stuff I remember from my undergraduate micro class!

Mises's work exemplified the spirit and sense of life missing from economics today. We don't revere dead economists to maintain their place in some academic hierarchy, or to satisfy an atavistic desire for an unchanging intellectual order. We revere them because their ideas still have purchase, because their work yields knowledge that is sorely needed today. We read them and promote them in order to understand the world as it is, filled with billions of purposeful but often irrational human actors. We need dead economists to save us from ourselves and to refute the stubborn myths of collectivism. We need them most of all because their work and their insights are far superior to those of most economists alive today. There is no New Economics, only new academic work which painstakingly advances the knowledge bequeathed to us.

V. Conclusion

Mises certainly lived his life with a certain quiet *élan*, even in the face of setbacks and slights that would enrage a lesser man. Through it all he maintained a quiet dignity and elegance reminiscent of Old Austria. Never giving up, never giving in, always turning to the next task with steady resolve, believing in his work when the world did not.

Of course Mises sometimes allowed himself to succumb to pessimism, which you know if you've read his memoirs. Anyone who lived through the Great War, who had to flee authoritarianism and uproot his life twice, who had to start over financially and otherwise in a new country, in a new language, who was treated so shabbily by the academic establishment, can be excused for this.

We don't have that excuse. We have the full body of Mises's work to read and enjoy, to guide us in our thoughts and actions today. We can read more Mises in 2020, and less throwaway news and political commentary. His work inspires and engages us in ways that saturated social media outlets, lightweight editorialists, and maudlin self-help literature do not. Let's face it: most articles, books, podcasts, and television shows today are not worthy of our time. Free online content is almost infinite today, but time surely is not.

Yes, there are very dark clouds on the horizon. Liberalism, the good and true version, never fully took hold in the West. And it's waning today. We shouldn't kid ourselves about this, or pretend otherwise. The West is politically illiberal today, and getting worse. But this does not counsel despair; it counsels us to summon our own sense of *élan vital*.